The Parish Handbook

Bob Mayo

with

Cameron Collington and the
Rt Revd David Gillett

scm press

To Sylvie

© Bob Mayo, 2016

First published in 2016 by SCM Press
Editorial office
3rd Floor, Invicta House,
108–114 Golden Lane,
London EC1Y 0TG

Hymns Ancient & Modern® is a registered trademark
of Hymns Ancient and Modern Ltd

SCM Press is an imprint of Hymns Ancient & Modern Ltd
(a registered charity)
13A Hellesdon Park Road, Norwich,
Norfolk, NR6 5DR, UK

www.scmpress.co.uk

British Library Cataloguing in Publication data

A catalogue record for this book is available
from the British Library

ISBN 978 0 334 05359 0

Typeset by Regent Typesetting
Printed and bound in Great Britain by
CPI Group (UK) Ltd

Contents

Preface

THE RT REVD DAVID GILLETT

One of my friends commented to me recently that being a parish priest must rank as one of the best jobs there is. Another, just a few days before, had told me he was thinking of giving up being a vicar as life had become unbelievably stressful!

If a person is thinking about being ordained both of those perspectives have to be considered. This book will be an enormous help in telling the story as it is and helping someone to make a mature and prayerful decision.

As the author mentions in the Introduction, I was his training incumbent when he was first ordained to serve as a curate in Luton. When I left that parish I became principal of a theological college. I often wondered in those years if anyone would write a book that could be given with confidence to those thinking about ordination or already in training – a book that would tell it as it is and also reveal the privilege and joy of being a parish priest. Here it is!

The author's approach moves from stories of real life to the stories and teaching of the Bible, and sometimes the other way round. The book is concerned to show that the lived experience of ministry today is part of the ongoing task of renewing a theology that is truthful and engaging. Theology is not something learned once and for all in the lecture room and by reading books, though both are important and valuable. Theology grows and is renewed as we seek to understand in Christ the real-life stories we encounter in others and ourselves.

A few months before I was ordained I came across a letter written by Evelyn Underhill to the Archbishop of Canterbury just before the Lambeth Conference of 1920. She was a much-valued spiritual director and writer on prayer in the early part of the last century. It made a deep impression on me and continues to do so today:

> We look to the Church to give us an experience of God, Mystery, Holiness, and Prayer, which shall lift us to contact the supernatural world – minister eternal life. We look to the clergy to help and direct our spiritual growth. We are seldom satisfied, because with a few noble exceptions they are so lacking in spiritual realism, so ignorant of the laws and experiences of the life of prayer. Their dealings with souls are often vague and amateurish. Those needing spiritual help may find much kindliness, but seldom that firm touch and first-hand knowledge of interior ways, which come only from a disciplined personal life of prayer. God is the interesting thing about religion. People are hungry for God. But only a priest whose life is soaked in prayer, sacrifice and love, can by his own spirit of adoring worship help us to apprehend Him. His secret correspondence with God – however difficult and apparently unrewarding – is the first duty of every priest.

This book certainly shows 'spiritual realism' combining, as it does, a deep empathy with the experience of all kinds of people in the author's urban parish and revealing many moments when God has become real in their lives. God is certainly 'the interesting thing' in this book – it is the story of God as it is lived out in the story of everyday parish life. We all begin in ministry with a lot that is still 'vague and amateurish'.

Thankfully this book is further on than that. There is professionalism here that delights in the process of learning the deeper ways of God and how Christ is brought to life in the tears and laughter of parish life. But it is not a professionalism that sets the author apart from the people he serves. It is one that gets involved with a wide range of people – from the sick and elderly to professional football players, from young people in rebellion against inherited patterns of society to the high-flying financier.

It is all too easy for books on parish ministry to offer definitive blueprints for the way forward. This handbook suggests that changes will come through the simplicity of us being able to reflect and learn together on what we have. It asks us to celebrate where we are before moving on to what we may become. The Church is an institution, but fundamentally she is the bride of Christ, fashioned by the Word to be the servant of all and God's emissary to the world.

Here the reader – be they training for ordination or well on in ministry – will find a joy in people, a confidence in the role of a parish priest, a faithfulness to the Scriptures and Christian tradition, all focused on the primary need of making Christ real in the lives of people and communities.

It is probably best to read this book by dipping into a chapter or two every day. Each one is a stand-alone piece of narrative theology, which is deceptively easy to read. Yet all will pay dividends if the reader reflects on Scripture and their own experience in the light of the particular subject being dealt with – and then seeks to bring that into the story of situations and individuals they know well. Along the way memorable phrases will take root and hopefully germinate later: 'The occasional offices are liquid gold', 'Conversion is a collision of narratives', 'Silences change a speech into a sermon and turn an audience into a congregation', 'A joyful parish church is fabulous and fragile'.

There are many more radical challenges for the parish priest to negotiate today than when I was ordained in the 1960s. But this book weaves its way realistically through these, and shows how there is very little else that gives as much opportunity for the gospel than when the priest is immersed in a locality with its inherited building and its rich diversity of people – to be known, loved and introduced to the love of God in Christ.

All in all, this book delights both in the opportunities of parish ministry and in the two-way dialogue between parish and theology. As that weaves into one cohesive story we discover more and more of the joys of what it means to minister in the name of Christ.

Introduction

The Parish Handbook looks at the ways in which parishes and local churches are a part of God's redemptive plan. Our mandate is simple. We are to take our stand humbly but decisively on the completed work of Christ upon the cross and to live faithfully in the world. The Church is in God's keeping and it is not for us to be anxious.

The work of *The Parish Handbook* owes a debt to the missionary thinking of Bishop Lesslie Newbigin who opened up outside-in ways of looking at Western culture and offered insights into how the Church can be recognized as acting out the story of God's love in the world. The vocation for a local church is to exercise a counter-cultural role in the community by bringing together different groups of people who might otherwise never have met. Parish churches are relevant to society precisely because of their non-conformity to contemporary culture. A parish church, that gathers people together from across the community, is a site of resistance against the increasingly atomized and segregated society in which we live. A parish church is built on the fragility of recently made relationships, the loyalty of the long-standing members, the poignancy of people greeting one another with the peace of Christ in the communion service and the possibilities represented in gathering people together in the name of Christ. A believing, celebrating and loving Christian congregation, rooted in Christ, committed to one another and invested in the life of the community will not be able to withhold from others the secret of its hope.

The Church has a passion for the ordinary and a vision for the expected. *The Parish Handbook* captures the imagination for what is possible. The book spells out the art of ordinary living, which is at the heart of parish life. Ordinary living in a parish means spending time visiting people in their homes and sharing in the routine of their lives. It means making relationships with a teenager as readily as an octogenarian, caring for the sick and dying, dealing with arguments, and helping people to cope with the failures of marriages and the loss of a child. It means celebrating birthdays, both happy and sad anniversaries, and planning Sunday services for people who prefer the traditional liturgy alongside others who are looking for something more contemporary.

The Church is a source of transformation for society offering the riches of Christian teaching, the resilience of Christian relationships, and the practice of Christian hope. The Church is the only public body in the community fully able to gather together at the same time different genders, ages, race and class. Brueggemann (2007, p. 52) says that the Church's work is the gathering of others, not the ones who belong obviously to our social tribe or class or race. If you look at a group of people and see no immediately apparent reason why they are together, then you are likely to be in a church.

There is nothing so capable of transforming people's lives as a church in love with Christ. The truth of Christ is Scripture revealed, tradition formed, community shaped and individually learnt. The mission of a parish church is to gather together people who might not otherwise have met. Young parents want assistance. Older people want companionship. Young people want encouragement. All want simple friendship while meeting together in the name of Christ.

Parishes form the bedrock of the Church of England's mission to the country and are still the heart of her identity in the community. Newbigin (1989) wrote, 'I do not think that we shall recover the true form of the parish until we recover a truly missionary approach to our culture. I don't think that we shall achieve a missionary encounter with our culture without recovering the true form of the parish.'

It has now officially been recognized that the best place for people of different cultures to meet is in a church. A 2014 report published by the Social Integration Commission identified that churches and other places of worship are more successful at bringing people of different backgrounds together than gatherings such as parties, meetings and weddings, or venues such as pubs and clubs. While spectator sports events are the most successful at bringing people of different ages together, churches are the most likely place for people from different cultures to meet.

The older inherited forms of church are relevant to society precisely because of their non-conformity to contemporary culture. 'Only connect!' said Margaret Schlegel in E. M. Forster's *Howards End*:

> That was the whole of her sermon. Only connect the prose and the passion, and both will be exalted, and human love will be seen at its height. Live in fragments no longer. Only connect and the beast and the monk, robbed of the isolation that is life to either, will die. Nor was the message difficult to give. It need not take the form of a good 'talking'. By quiet indications the bridge would be built and span their lives with beauty.

Trinity

Generally, the Trinity does not hold a central place in the liturgical year of the parish. In a parish liturgical year the clergy will celebrate Christmas, ignore eschatology and struggle with the Trinity. They are in good company in doing so. Augustine (*De Trin* V, 9 VII.4) admitted that he used the term 'Trinity' for want of anything else to say – to call God what is meant by 'person' is simply a necessity or protocol for speaking.

The Trinity is seen as a troublesome piece of theological baggage best kept out of the way when talking about the faith to non-believers and is most easily explained in a Trinity Sunday sermon by using the analogy of water, ice and steam, three leaves of a shamrock, or different notes of music – each entirely separate but of the same substance. A sermon simply demonstrating that a three in one God is possible falls a long way short of showing how it shapes our identity as the people of God. Church leaders apologize on behalf of the Trinity to their congregations, telling them that the doctrine is hard to understand. They talk about the 'doctrine of the Trinity' rather than simply 'the Trinity'.

Okechukwu Ogbonnaya (1998) writes that the Trinity has long

been considered an enigma within Western Christendom because a Communitarian Divinity does not fit with our individualized, self-referential, consumer rights-driven worldview. Christianity in the last analysis is trinitarian. Take out of the New Testament the persons of Father, Son and Holy Spirit and there is no God left. Church life without the Trinity is like having the ingredients without the recipe to put them all together.

The parish church is Trinity shaped. Each church has a story to tell, a fellowship to build, and a mission to pursue. The Father's love is the story we tell through our witness and evangelism (Eph. 4.6). The Son's service is the mission we follow in service and love for the local community (Luke 19.10). The Holy Spirit's fellowship is the root of the relationships we form as the body of Christ (2 Cor. 13.14). Each feeds into and out of the other.

Narrative theology

The Parish Handbook is a book of narrative theology. This is looked at in more detail later in the book (N – Narrative theology). A narrative approach to the Bible makes theology a collective enterprise, equipping the Church with the understandings and insights to read through, live, and pray out the stories of Scripture. The stories are there to be shared and they are the places of encounter between the community and God.

The handbook is not a church manual with tips on evangelism, thoughts on people management or directions on liturgy. It is not a how-to book or an individual call to action. It is an invitation to us all to celebrate the Church, an organism as well as an organization, beating with the living heart of Christ.

There are a series of books written on parishes that talk about how much parishes need to change and why a particular book offers the key to how this might be done – in other words, if they can identify something as a problem, then they can put themselves forward as the solution. *The Parish Handbook* takes a different approach. Changes will come through the simplicity of us being able to reflect, learn together, and celebrate where we are now before moving on to what we may become. As T. S. Eliot writes, 'home is where one starts from . . . a lifetime burning in every moment'. The Church is an institution, but she is also the bride of Christ, servant of all, and God's emissary to the world.

Dreamer disciple and revolutionary

A Christian is a dreamer disciple and revolutionary. When Joel (2.28) says that old men will dream dreams and young men will see visions, he is not talking about what is practical or possible, but what is imaginable. As I open the church doors on a Sunday morning I dream of the world's rejuvenation at Christ's return: 'The wolf will live with the lamb, the leopard will lie down with the goat, the calf and the lion and the yearling together; and a little child will lead them' (Isa. 11.6).

My daily discipleship is fuelled by this eschatological vision. When I put the rubbish out after church for collection on a Monday morning I am living out the dislocation between the ways of God and of society. As a revolutionary I rejoice in the future hope of God's coming presence in the world (Rom. 5.2). The raison d'être of the Church is to draw attention to Christ's return and to live it out as her way of being in the world. A church is a dialogical presence at the heart of a community, pointing to an eschatological reality beyond.

The Church is a prophetic minority, not a moral majority. Coming together in the name of Christ is an act of hope in which we imagine how the world would be different to how it is were the Kingdom of God here on earth. We act as if it could be, and then find that in so doing it is becoming so. In a Church built on the resurrected Christ, ideas shape energy, imagination shapes organization, possibility shapes pragmatism. Sociologist David Martin writes that if the Church does not concern itself with mystery, transcendence and worship, then it might as well pack up and go home (Martin, 2002, p. 140).

The tolling of the church bells on Sunday morning, calling people to worship, represents the universal Church to the particular parish and also the particular to the universal. As parish churches act out the life of Christ in their local communities, they are speaking with the weight of 2,000 years of history behind them and 2.1 billion Christians worldwide alongside them.

Writing the book

I owe a debt of gratitude to the missionary thinking of Bishop Lesslie Newbigin, who opened up outside-in ways of looking at Western culture and offered insights into how the Church can be recognized as acting out the story of God's love in the world. During the writing of this book God gave me a thorn in the flesh to keep me humble (2 Cor. 12.7), but also congregations at St Stephens and St Michaels to keep me hopeful. I have had privileges afforded to few. I have seen a friendship develop between a 99-year-old and a 10-year-old who, apart from at church, would likely have never met each other. I have taken the funeral of two men who lived ten doors apart but never properly met, and then to be able to introduce their widows to each other. I have talked with an ex-serviceman who landed on the D Day beaches when he was only 17. He was in the SAS during the war and is still reticent to talk about all that happened.

There are 26 chapters in this book, each beginning with a letter of the alphabet and each covering an aspect of parish life. Every chapter concludes with a reflection and a prayer, most of which are from the Revd Cameron Collington, vicar in the parish next door to mine. The final word goes to the Rt Revd David Gillett, my original training incumbent and, since then, Principal of Trinity Theological College and Bishop of Bolton. David has written the conclusion to this book. The fact of our collaboration is a statement of principle that theology belongs to the café, the living room and the pub as much as to the theological academy.

Jesus had 30 years to prepare for three years of public ministry. For the parish clergy it is the reverse. We have no more than three years at theological college to prepare for over 30 years of ministry. Our discipleship springs from praxis-based theology, a combination of reflection and action. Our life-long learning requires an ongoing dialogue between the academy and the field. The two meet together in the parish where each has to make sense of the other. The knowledge of the academy and the practical experience from the field join together in the worshipping congregation.

In parish life the age of partisan denominationalism has passed and a new period of integrated churchmanship lies open before us. Alpha courses are everywhere. Inclusivity and same-sex relationships are here to stay. A new bishop is as likely to be female as male. Social diversity is represented in congregations, if not yet in church leadership. It is a 'dog helps dog' world, says my brother Edward Mayo (2010). Congregation members have left their pews to pioneer fresh expressions of Church. It is now time for the parish church to rediscover its radical authentic missionary self.

Prologue

Homeless people come frequently to my door. Andy set up a tent for himself under the bicycle racks and stayed for a month. Sam came straight from prison, having been let out with nowhere to go. Barry came wanting to end his life, though I did not realize this till afterwards.

It was blisteringly hot. He lay under the tree at the front of our house, matted with sweat and dirt and did not move. We brought him chicken and chips in the evening and bacon sandwiches in the morning, but he would eat neither and the unopened packets lay stacked beside him. We gave him water so that he could at least rehydrate himself. He lay in a tinder-dry pile of leaves and smoked. It was a Health and Safety nightmare.

People in Barry's position generally want to talk. They are bitter, hungry or lonely and want to speak about what has happened to them. Barry was numbed and told me nothing about his situation.

On the third night I sat with him by the tree. I stayed past midnight and held him like a child as he cried. Tears appeared on the edge of his eyes, but never reached the bottom of his cheeks because they were absorbed into the dirt and sweat matted on to his face. Still he said nothing, but it was important that I was there.

My short time sitting with Barry is a part of the wider pattern of God's love for the world: '... through the dark and empty desolation', wrote T. S. Eliot, 'love is most nearly itself when here and now cease to matter' (Eliot, 2001).

The next day Sylvie and I were able finally to persuade Barry to take a shower. That night his wallet was stolen. The combination of having had a shower and his wallet stolen jolted him out of his stupor. The shower cleaned him up and gave him back a sense of dignity and responsibility for the man he was. The stolen wallet lent urgency to his situation.

Barry admitted to me that he had a place in a hostel in the Midlands. I paid for his ticket and put him on the next train home. I rang the staff at the hostel and learnt of what had been Barry's intention in coming to London – he had disappeared from the hostel and left a suicide message on their answerphone. He had chosen the cosy hidden space between the tree and the front vicarage wall to end his days.

He met a fine group of people who helped to restore him to life. Sylvie, my wife, was project manager. Rudi can charm the birds out of the trees, but then will worry about them afterwards; Chris will have thought of a solution before he knows the problem; Anne will listen with the patience of the angels to people in distress.

Ruth Etchelles's poem 'The Judas Tree' tells about Judas, in hell, hanging on the tree of his own despair. Jesus cuts Judas down from the tree and takes him in his arms: 'It was for this I came, he said and not to do you harm' (Etchelles, 1972).

All over the country there are people in parishes cutting others down from their own individual Judas trees by telling them the story of Christ's love and forgiveness. Christianity is not based on time-transcending ideas, but is rooted in particular events in recorded history. In looking after Barry we were simply carrying on the 2,000-year-old story of the Church in society.

A

Alone

When I stand up to preach, it is always with the same sensation. I am Isaiah in the temple or Peter falling at Jesus' knees saying 'Go away from me, Lord; I am a sinful man!' (Isa. 6; Luke 5.8). The reality of God is an uncomfortable truth. As I start my sermon it is always 'midnight' and the 'bridegroom' is in sight, yet the 'wise virgins' will still not share their oil in case they are left without enough for themselves (Matt. 25.1–13). On that night two people will be in one bed; one will be taken and the other left (Luke 17.34).

I am like one of the 'virgins' at midnight in Jesus' parable. I can tell people of the coming Christ but I can't myself pass on to them the 'oil' of God's grace. Each person has to receive it himself or herself as a gift straight from the Lord. This truth contains within it the paradox of Christian leadership. I can teach, encourage and witness to the love of Christ, but my effectiveness in so doing comes in drawing attention away from myself. As with John the Baptist: 'He must become greater; I must become less' (John 3.30).

There is a stamp of separation that lies at the heart of a life of faith in God. In the Old Testament God calls his people to a nomadic life of faith full of inconvenience and risk. Moses spent 40 years leading the Israelites through the wilderness on a journey that, if they had taken a different route, might otherwise have taken only 11 days (Ex. 13.17; Deut. 1.2). The generation of Israelites who left Egypt were not those who would start in the Promised Land :'The LORD's anger burned against Israel and he made them wander in the wilderness for forty years, until the whole generation of those who had done evil in his sight was gone' (Num. 32.13).

Moses brought the Israelites to the threshold of the Promised Land, but was not allowed by God to enter with them (Num.

20.9–11). David describes himself as lonely and afflicted (Ps. 25.16). Jeremiah (20.14) and Job (3.1) are driven to despair by what God is asking of them. They both curse the day on which they were born.

The disciples leave their families and shake the dust off their feet when people do not listen to them (Matt. 10.14; 19.29). Jesus then begins to distance himself from them as they walk towards Jerusalem, and he walks ahead of them. They are astonished and afraid (Mark 10.32). Jesus has had a lifetime of being misunderstood (Matt. 13.55–56). He needs to face his coming trial alone and he is starting the process of separating himself from his disciples. In Gethsemane Jesus is in anguish: sweat was like drops of blood falling to the ground (Luke 22.44).

The need for separation and solitude is an integral part of being a church leader. Prayer, reading and reflection all require times of being alone; these are core roles for any church leader. The challenge for the church leader is to practise the art of solitude while avoiding the trap of loneliness. Solitude is something we choose. It is constructive and restorative. Loneliness is imposed. Tillich (2010) writes that loneliness expresses the pain of being alone, and solitude the glory of being alone. In a society that puts a premium on romantic love and relationships, solitude is not properly appreciated. Solitude can be as therapeutic and insightful as can emotional support and friendship from others.

Loneliness in the parish

Rowan Williams (1995, p. 121) wrote that Christians seem to treat the subject of loneliness with a consistent lack of seriousness and with a painful lack of imagination and sympathy. What the Bible depicts as prayer reflects the often lonely experience of the parish priest. Prayer is, in effect, an offering to God of our obedience. The fundamental truth is that Christ's way is the way of self-emptying (Phil. 2.5–11). It is a way that the world sees as weakness and failure. The day-to-day living of the parish priest, poured out in conversations, prayer and 'stick-at-it-ness', makes it a necessary truth to learn that Christ took no account of achievement and success, only of serving, giving and loving.

The possibility of loneliness is never far away for a church leader. There is a hard edge to living in a vicarage and being permanently accessible to others. I can only lose when someone knocks at the door asking for money. If I give the person money then it is no more than what is expected of me. If I do not do so then I am open to criticism for being ungenerous. I have nights with people ringing the vicarage door at 2 a.m. and then again at 5 a.m. At the church school fete it is seen as obligatory for the vicar to buy a raffle ticket, but it is equally as important that he is never seen to win the prize.

My loneliness has the stamp of the Beatitudes. The Beatitudes are a text of beauty and terror. We are blessed for being poor in spirit, mourning, being insulted or persecuted (Matt. 5.3–12). We are left clean with an inner raw longing for God. There is nowhere to hide when leading public worship. I preach as someone longing for God. I pray as someone reaching out for God. I sing as someone praising God and lead others in the process.

Loneliness can be a channel of grace and the grace of God makes us who we are (1 Cor. 15.10). Nouwen (1997) writes that loneliness can be not only tolerable, but also fruitful. Some of the most diligent, conscientious and devoted ministers that I have known have been celibate with a hint of loneliness. Freed from the exclusive attachments of family, they are able to be available to God and to meet with people as one vulnerable person to another. 'I wish that all of you were as I am', says Paul of his unmarried state, 'but each of you has your own gift from God; one has this gift, another has that' (1 Cor. 7.7). The gospel takes shape through people's weakness and vulnerability. Paul talks thus about the pressures he faced through his own public ministry: 'We are hard pressed on every side, but not crushed; perplexed, but not in despair; persecuted, but not abandoned; struck down, but not destroyed' (2 Cor. 4.8–9).

Sometimes the greatest cause of isolation is not what others do, but what we do to ourselves. Warren (2002) and Savage (2006) both say that clergy are stressed because they are carrying around unreasonable expectations of themselves, and disappointed because the reality of parish life has not lived up to the ideal they had imagined. A difficult individual, an unresolved issue, or a lack of gratitude for what we do are not issues peculiar to a parish but would be evident in any number of work contexts.

Parish work can feel like a treadmill where clergy are left struggling to keep up with what they feel are endless demands made on their time. A sense of isolation can be exacerbated by the fact that there is an assumed competence to the role of church leader whose task is to care for others. It is possible to be with people and still feel isolated.

Friendship-forming is a critical role for the Church to play. Set against a social backdrop of rural isolation, urban fragmentation and suburban commuting, parish churches offer people a chance to gather together and to form relationships with one another. Our strength as the Church lies in our collective relationships in the name of Jesus Christ. Our uniqueness lies in the one true historical faith. Our mission is to embody this in how we live our lives, shaping ourselves round the needs of the most vulnerable because therein lies the face of Christ.

In the Old Testament David and Jonathan's friendship had started when each recognized the courage in the other. Before he fought Goliath, David had fought a lion and a bear (1 Sam. 17.34). Jonathan himself was a man of great courage. He had initiated a one-man war against the Philistines (1 Sam. 14). Jonathan accepted God's decision that David, rather than he, should be king. At Jonathan's funeral David wept and described Jonathan's love as more wonderful than that of women (2 Sam. 1.26).

Loneliness in Scripture

The paradox of Christianity is that God's power is made perfect in weakness. The trauma of crucifixion contains within it the offer of salvation. The brokenness of one is the salvation of all. The importance of Jesus' cry of despair from the cross is shown in the fact that only one of Jesus' seven sayings from the cross is recorded in both Mark and Matthew: 'My God, my God, why have you forsaken me?' (Mark 15.34; Matt. 27.46). It comes after Jesus has been on the cross for six hours. It contains within it the insight needed for those difficult weeks you have as a church leader. Jesus' words come from Psalm 22. The Psalm is in two parts: verses 1–21 (suffering and grief) and verses 22–31 (praise and hope). Hope and grief are not binary opposites but are each a part of the other. Grieving does not happen automatically. Anyone can decide to cover up his pain and ignore unresolved grief. When we accept grief, we are choosing hope. Grieving embraced is a hopeful and deliberate choice, made because we want to be whole once more.

Psalm 22 bridges Jesus' crucifixion and resurrection, crossing from grief to hope. Jesus was alone, but not lonely. To think of Jesus as lonely stresses his human qualities: compassion, love, justice and social conscience and so on, at the expense of his divine nature. Jesus was temporarily lower than the angels (Heb. 2.9). This, however, was subservience in role but not subservience in essence. Jesus was not just someone chosen by God to do a special mission. Jesus was God himself.

Loneliness in society

We live in a lonely society. According to the 2015 report *Church in Action*, published by the Church Urban Fund (CUF), clergy listed loneliness and social isolation as the most widespread social problems affecting English communities, regardless of income or social class. The report showed that nearly half, or 46 per cent, of churches are running organized activities to tackle social isolation through programmes such as youth groups, parent and toddler groups or lunch clubs. Churches are also providing informal support, through social networks and friendship groups.

I spend time with people who live lonely lives. I go a short distance from the vicarage to the supermarket to buy a lunchtime sandwich. It takes me three attempts to return home, because on each occasion a homeless person asks for the sandwich that I have just bought for myself. They want companionship more than food and so I take time to speak to each of them in turn. It is Psalm 22 in the parish, but a lot easier for me with simple conversations than it had been for Jesus with his crucifixion.

Reflection

I put down the Bible after I read Mark 10.45: 'For even the Son of Man did not come to be served, but to serve, and to give his life as a ransom for many.'

I meditate on these words for many minutes, my lips moving silently over the words. This is a significant moment in a short time of solitude. I have had days of sermon preparation, shifting church tables, liaising with the Bishop about a confirmation service, and unplanned encounters. All are a heavy tax on the time and the emotions that I give to the parish.

A supportive PCC and encouragement at home are great assets, but as I linger on these words from Scripture, I think of moments where there are no teams or helpers on stand-by and the mantle for the occasion must be carried by me alone. The Holy Spirit draws me to the heart of it all. I feel that I have enough oil in my lamp to last at least another day.

Prayer

Lord God, thank you for calling me to the glory of solitude, and within my vocation as a priest to take time to walk alongside your people. Move me in the pattern of your example as I take on the regular ordeal of cross-shaped loneliness to point others to the oil of your healing and forgiveness. Amen.

B

Baptism

Baptism in society

Infant baptisms are subversive. Just as John the Baptist overturned people's expectations in calling the Pharisees to order (Matt. 3.1–2), so also does the current parish practice of a baptism, in offering to families the opportunity for a socially constructed celebration of their child's birth acted out in the context of a trinitarian statement of belief.

Parents and godparents are asked whether they 'turn to Christ', 'repent of their sins' and 'renounce evil'. The explicit Christian language within the service linked to a strong pedagogical preparation for the parents means that the baptism service becomes both an occasion for celebration and an opportunity for teaching the Christian faith. It is radical and traditional at the same time. It fulfils the parents' desire for a ceremony to mark the birth of their child and society's expectations of the Church while also creating the opportunity for the Church to teach the Christian faith to the baptism families.

Bob Jackson (2002) writes that churches only seem to be growing overall in attendance where they have a fairly high proportion of children. He says that this suggests a priority church-growth aim of focusing on children, young people and families. Such is the kinship of first-time parents to be in the company of others in the same situation that baptism courses for groups of parents wanting their child baptized become a de facto post-natal class. People swap stories about the realities of their lives as new parents. Offering to baptize their children is a key missionary tool for the Church to be able to engage with the local community.

For us, a three-evening baptism course with three families together is no more work than it would be to meet with a single family for one evening. Baptism courses for groups of parents wanting their child baptized bring social energy to theological learning. The parents' idealism at a new child, tinged with the panic at their new responsibility and the radical change in their social identity, makes a group glad to be together and keen to learn.

Across the UK there has been a decline in the number of people wanting baptism either for themselves or else for their children. Lloyd, Earey and Tarrant (2007) tell us that in the 1930s 70 per cent of all children were baptized into the Church of England. In the 1980s this figure had fallen to 30 per cent and in 2005 it was 15 per cent. While the numbers for baptisms may have decreased, people's reasons for seeking baptism are stronger than in previous generations because they are doing so out of personal choice rather than social obligation.

Infant baptisms are a celebration. Baptisms remain abidingly popular among parents because there is no other public occasion with the weight and significance of a baptism to celebrate the birth of a child. The celebration lunch after the baptism in church is not just relaxation after the main event, but an indication that there is a dual focal lens to the process. This offers to parents both a social occasion for them to introduce their child to the wider family, as well as a church ceremony for them to mark the birth of their child before God. As families often live some distance apart, the former is important as is also the latter.

Baptisms are the new weddings. As more people opt for 'merger marriage' in their thirties rather than 'start up' marriage in their twenties, the social significance of baptism is enhanced. Marriage has ceased to be the rite of passage that it has been in previous generations, and so it is their child's baptism rather than their own marriage that marks the change in people's lifestyle. If a couple have been living together before they are married, as is increasingly common, then marriage will simply confirm the life choices that they have already made. Once a month I would have a 'baptism jubilee'. Families would gather in a celebratory mood, children crowd round as water is tipped from a height into the font, and parents are congratulated afterwards on what they have achieved.

A part of the continuing appeal of baptism services is the opportunity for parents to draw in friends and family as godparents.

The numbers nationally for baptisms may have decreased, but the number of godparents per child has increased. Godparents play a role in creating contemporary households out of traditional families. Thatcher (2007, p. 133) refers to the practice of gathering multiple adults round the parenting of a child as 'blended families'. A baptismal group of parents, friends, relatives and godparents form one such example of how this might be.

Missionary engagement

The occasional offices are liquid gold in terms of their missionary outreach, if not always done in what might previously have been a set order. People may want a christening service to precede, follow or even to be a part of their wedding ceremony. Family ties, in the sense of husband or wife, are no longer a matter of course but a freely chosen act, based on feelings and personal harmony. Marriage needs to prove itself as the best option against a horizon of different possibilities. Adults may marry, divorce, cohabit or live singly.

A christening is a part of a natural process of parenthood initiating children into a wider family narrative. Being a part of a family is telling stories about one another and making children aware of the history of which they are a part:

> I think that we should not admire religious or non-religious parents who are afraid to share their values and convictions with their children. It is a false and bad-faith position to think that if we do not teach them values our children will be free to make up their own minds (Hauerwas, 1981, p. 166).

A decision by the Church to baptize children is an act of missionary generosity more than one of theological orthodoxy. Infant baptism is an act of doctrinal hospitality from the Church towards parents who are drawn to the Church searching for a formal public context to mark the birth of their child. Infant baptism is a staging post along the way in the process of the parents and godparents developing an awareness of the grace of God and moving towards a conscious Christological response.

Baptism in the Bible

Adult baptism is in essence the sign of God's work in a person's heart and the seal of someone's response in faith. Going into the water and coming up out of it symbolizes the baptized person coming through the muddle and chaos of human sin into the love and delight of the Father.

A person who comes forward for baptism is aware of the chaos and muddle both in and around them and is willing to be baptized into this disorder in order to be raised up to meet with Christ. Rowan Williams (2014) asks where might you expect to find the baptized? He answers in the neighbourhood of chaos in his own life. A baptized person is both in the middle of human threat, suffering and pain, and in the middle of the joy and delight of the Father.

In the Old Testament children are always seen as a part of a family and are included in God's wider blessing. God makes a family-covenant: he will be the God of believers and also of their children (Gen. 17.7). In the New Testament, Lydia, the Philippian jailer and Stephanus brought forward their whole households for baptism (Acts 16.15, 33; 1 Cor. 1.16). These examples suggest that household baptisms were a common practice. There is no reason to suppose that there were no young children in any of them and that the parents were not making a decision on their behalf.

In the Old Testament God's revelation is wider than the Israelites. God reveals himself to unlikely people such as Rahab the prostitute (Josh. 6.25). In the New Testament God's revelation is wider than just to the Jews. Jesus shows himself to the Syro-Phoenician woman (Matt. 15.21–28) and to the Roman centurion (Matt. 8.10).

When Jesus says that no one can come to the Father except through him (John 14.6), he is referring to himself not only as the incarnate Christ, but also as the pre-existent Logos, drawing people towards him through the work of the Holy Spirit. As we proclaim the 'mystery of our faith' during the baptism service we are recognizing that God is responding to his own image in those gathered for baptism. The water of baptism is a symbol of new life. The liturgy of baptism is an acknowledgement of us being created 'in the image of God'.

Infant baptism stresses the grace of God while adult baptism emphasizes the redemption of the believer. Jesus' was the proto-type adult baptism coming up out of the water to receive the Holy Spirit and to hear a voice from heaven that said, 'This is my Son, whom I love' (Matt. 3.17). Jesus speaks of the suffering and death that lies ahead of him as a baptism that he is going to endure (Mark 10.38). Paul speaks of being baptized by means of the power of the Holy Spirit in the death and resurrection of Jesus Christ (Rom. 6.3–5).

On Sunday as I welcome people to church I am both guest and host in our Christ-scarred society. How do I hear the voice of Christ through the different voices of people wanting their child baptized for a variety of reasons that are not immediately apparent? It is not my role to police people's intentions in bring-ing a child forward for baptism. It is not my position to construct a watertight hermeneutic of the gospel based solely on the cog-nitive awareness of those involved in the ceremony. In a baptism ceremony the orthodoxy lies in the liturgy. This gives me the free-dom to offer to the parents the same generosity of spirit shown by Paul writing from prison in Philippi: 'The important thing is that in every way, whether from false motives or true, Christ is preached. And because of this I rejoice' (Phil. 1.18).

Reflection

It is a Saturday afternoon and I am driving to pick up my wife and our newborn from hospital. I am impatient about the scores of football fans, including mini-kitted babes in arms, jaywalking in front of me, causing traffic delays. Children in the football colours of their parents' team give me a sharp moment of illumination. Their happy faces provide a new insight into the vital role of infant baptism within the Church. The children are being inducted into the parents' story of the world. One day they would have the freedom to follow another outfit, but for now they are part of what the family are doing, and apparently with great juvenile joy.

Prayer

Heavenly Father, thank you for my baptismal vows. As I recall them, continue to draw me to you, the bringer of order to the chaos in this world. I thank you for the missionary opportunity of baptism. Help me to direct all those who come for baptism straight to the love of your Son, our Lord Jesus Christ. Amen.

C

Conversation

Conversation is at the heart of the Christian faith: a transcendental God and a mortal man require dialogue and mediation at its centre. The Church echoes the Psalmist's lament over the state of sin, adopts the prophetic critique of sinful behaviour, and opens up the transformative possibility of a new life in Christ. The greatest joy in heaven is over the one sinner who repents and begins that process of discovery for themselves (Luke 15.7).

Jesus is an educator and in our evangelical selves we become one too. There are three educational styles that Jesus adopts in his conversations with people. Each has resonance with us in how we talk about the Christian faith. Conversation is an art and not a science, and hence the approaches overlap rather than remain distinct. In his conversations Jesus was either dispassionate, dialogical or direct.

Dispassionate informal education

The dispassionate nature of a church leader's role is shown during the times when people need to be supported in critically reflecting on their own experiences and reaching their own conclusions, be this with reference to the faith or not. A young person at school, a widow recently bereaved, or parents with a young child all need space and opportunity to explore new and different ways of being in the world. It is a type of informal education and is more common practice for youth workers than for clergy. Informal learning happens naturally at the edges of the churches with parent and toddler groups, old and young people's clubs, and provision for the homeless. People are offered practical support, friendship and opportunities for thinking and reflection.

Jesus was direct with the rich young ruler when he told him to sell all that he had and give it to the poor. Jesus was dispassionate as he watched the rich young ruler walk away and did not follow him to try to persuade him to change his mind (Matt. 19.16–26). Jesus remains dispassionate on the occasions when he needs to maintain a clear focus on his mission and to avoid getting caught up in other people's expectations. One such example is when he said to the Canaanite woman that he was sent only to the lost sheep of Israel (Matt. 15.24).

Jesus tries to remain dispassionate and to avoid being drawn in by people's preconceptions and being falsely labelled as the powerful political Messiah that people want him to be. Jesus heals people, but tells them to keep quiet about what has happened to them (Mark 1.41–44). He could see how early publicity about his miracles would hinder his mission. People would come to him wanting to see what he could do for them rather than to hear what he had to say. He was right. When the leper talked openly about his healing, such large crowds began to follow Jesus that he could not enter towns openly (Mark 1.45).

The strange elusive nature of Christian truth is such that Jesus makes no claim to be the Messiah when confronted by the 5,000-strong crowd that he had fed, nor by the cheering crowd as he enters Jerusalem. After the feeding of the 5,000, Jesus would have had the crowd hanging on to his every word if he had started to talk of himself as the Messiah. He knew that if he did so it would have left people hoping for the overthrow of the Romans, and so he refrained. They would have come to him by force to make him king and so he withdrew by himself to a mountain (John 6.15).

Jesus does the same thing after his entry into Jerusalem as he had done after the feeding of the 5,000. He withdraws to be on his own (Mark 11.11). It is only when he is on trial in front of the Sanhedrin that Jesus confirms his identity as the Son of God:

Again the high priest asked him, 'Are you the Messiah, the Son of the Blessed One?'

'I am,' said Jesus. 'And you will see the Son of Man sitting at the right hand of the Mighty One and coming on the clouds of heaven' (Mark 14.61–62).

The Sanhedrin condemns him and the events leading towards his death are set in motion. Jesus resists the temptation to be the 'stones into bread', 'jumping from a high place', 'kingdoms of the world' Messiah (Matt. 4.1–11). What the Father asks of the Son is to accept the reality of his situation and not to play to the crowd. Jesus is not going to bypass the hostility of the temple authorities, but is going to live with the reality of how things are even if it results in his death.

What the Father asks of us is to learn to live and attend to the reality of the Church as it is, to do the prosaic things that can and must be done now, and to work at our relationships with the people who will not listen to us – or may not even like us: 'The hardest thing in the world is to be where we are in the confusion and complexity of the present moment' (Williams, 2000, pp. 85–6).

Dialogical non-formal education

There is an ongoing dialogue with God through the Psalms and Prophets as to why the wicked prosper. Abraham and God dialogue together over the fate of Sodom and Gomorrah (Gen. 18.16–33). Hosea marries a promiscuous woman to represent the behaviour shown by the Israelites towards God (Hos. 1.2). The fact of there being a dialogue between God and mankind does not mean that the outcome is altered, in the sense it was necessarily firmly fixed in the first place, so much as worked out as a new reality between God and the person interceding.

Examples of dialogue in the Old Testament are revealed in the New Testament as being a part of the essential nature of God's interaction with people. Jesus asks a Samaritan woman to give him some water from a nearby well and tells her that if she had known whom she was talking to she would have asked for living water (John 4.10). The encounter is startling because Jesus is breaking two social conventions: he is a Jew speaking to a Samaritan and a rabbi talking to a woman.

Jesus does not condemn the woman caught in adultery (John 8.11) but starts a dialogue, with those who bring her to him, on the nature of sin. Drawing in the sand while they wait for him to speak is his way of taking the heat out of the situation. It is an interactive method of encouraging the accusers to reflect on their position – figures in the sand can be reshaped in the same way that ideas can be revised, and that is what he is encouraging the woman's accusers to do. It is a high-risk strategy. The woman would presumably have preferred Jesus simply to tell her accusers not to throw stones at her.

Historically, Bible listening would have been more common than Bible reading. The idea of Bible reading as a person sitting alone in a room reading a leather-bound volume is a modern construct. The Scriptures would be read out to groups of people who would then talk together about what it meant. I have this experience for myself when working with the Church of South India. There is a church for which we have responsibility but little opportunity to visit. We pay a Hindu lady to read Scripture each week at the same time and in the same place in the village. She is one of the few people in the village who is able to read. She is not a Christian and the people in the village have no biblical background. When we visit the village we find groups of people talking together about the meaning of what they have had read to them.

Jesus is dialogical when he tells parables, inviting his listeners into a discussion about what the story means. The central theme to the Parable of the Sower is that most of what is said is lost and hence why the generative power of story-telling lends itself to evangelism. Stories appeal to people's imagination rather than having to rely solely on their comprehension. Stories draw people into a conversation about the nature of meaning: how one interprets a story is indicative of what one thinks of as important.

The light and fuel of a parish church's mission lies in the energy and creativity of its story-telling. The stories people tell of themselves, their workplace and home lives, and their relationship with God, are the crown jewels of parish evangelism:

> People's stories also matter to them [young people], stories that fill conversations. Television shows, movies, Facebook and Twitter – why have we often given them clichéd propositions and empty programs when the sharing of stories in the context of God's story is so dynamic? (Borgman, 2013, p. 52).

The task of mission and evangelism is to connect the story of Jesus Christ with the many different narratives in which people live their lives and through which they find purpose and meaning. Conversion is a collision of narratives. The Christian story is formational as well as informational. When we tell the gospel story we are inviting those listening to read themselves into the narrative and to take part in its outworking.

For the Christian, the story of Jesus is the story par excellence. It is God's way of being with human beings. It offers dialogue and invites interaction between God and mankind. We are shaped as the people of God by stories and metaphors and not by habits and rules of behaviour. We don't just learn the story; we *become* the story. Evangelism comes when we choose to share our stories with others so that they too can decide whether or not they want to keep it as their own. This radical goal, which concerns how one person becomes like another person, through the intermingling of stories, becomes the ultimate aim of our evangelism. Evangelism seeks to bring together the Christian story, and individuals' own stories.

Simkins (1977) describes a dialogical rather than propositional approach to truth as a non-formal education – this is formal material taught in an informal manner. Non-formal education serves its place in Alpha courses and small house groups. Hospitality and teaching, relationships and learning overlap with one another. Teaching is direct while conversation is non-hierarchical and interactive. People listen to the talk, giving a clear direction to their evening. They are able to explore the Christian faith in groups, discussing with others its significance and meaning.

Alpha courses often simply start the dialogue and are the beginning of a process that will lead towards a person coming to faith in Christ. The finding in a study by Hunt (2003) showed that it could take up to four years to feel fully established as a Christian.

Directional formal education

Jesus was direct with people when he wanted them to hear the unvarnished truth. He called the Pharisees whitened tombs (Matt. 23.27). He challenged people to repent and follow him. He taught in the synagogues proclaiming the good news of the Kingdom (Matt. 4.17–23). When he returned to Nazareth he declared that the words of the prophet Isaiah had been fulfilled (Luke 4.22–30).

The sermon is an obvious example of where a direct approach is appropriate. The sermon is the central plank of the church's week-by-week teaching. Simkins (1977) describes this as formal education whereby there is a curriculum to be taught and lessons to be learnt.

Equally, there are situations in conversation when directness is required. I have occasion to be so when away from the parish for three months on sabbatical. On my return, a couple with whom I had previously had a counselling-type relationship ask me to visit. They launch straight into an argument. They go through the issues that we had dealt with previously and then, as if perfectly choreographed, stop on cue, turn towards me, and wait for me to respond. They have sat on their disagreements waiting for my return, and now look to me for direction. My service to them is to be gentle in tone but direct in application in how I reply.

At his ascension Jesus ends with a direct call to action: make disciples (Matt. 28.19). After his resurrection Jesus appeared to more than 500 people at the same time (1 Cor. 15.6), yet only the original disciples witnessed his last moments on earth, one of whom had betrayed him and some of whom still doubted him. Like the disciples, we are the vulnerable ones, charged with Jesus' authority, living out the story of the resurrected Christ and bearing witness to his name, as the hope for the world.

Reflection

In order for Jim to take his place in the story of God, I judge that a 'direct' approach from me is not going to work. Instead, with much prayer and many coffees in the parish, I enjoy the friendship, working gently and being dispassionate about opening up the subject of God. We dialogue together in our conversations about the divine. Increasingly, he wants to start discussions about Christ and the benefits of having faith in him. In time, he asks me questions and seems to relish what he jokingly calls 'education sessions with the Vic'.

One day, Jim announces, with an air of ownership, that he is making a deal with God about his life. If God writes off all the bad stuff, he in turn will live differently from before. He moves back to be with his wife from whom he is estranged and introduces her to the story of Christ. After careful deliberation, she joins him in his new story of faith. Together Jim and his wife make life commitments to follow Jesus.

Prayer

Ever-loving God, thank you for your invitation to me to dialogue with you. I praise you for your grace, which lays before me the direct challenge of the cross. As I walk with you, sometimes stumbling, falling behind, or even looking away, pick me up and fill me with your life-giving Spirit – that I may discern the appropriate type of conversation for drawing each new individual into your story. Amen.

D

Death

Experiences of death

In *Hamlet*, Rosencratz declares 'an old man is twice a child'. We are a child when we are born and a child when we die. Larry was one such person. He was 92. He had landed on the D Day beaches as a teenager. He used to tell me of the excitement that everyone had felt. In the last hours before he died, his breath was rasping and his body was rigid. I held his head in my arms. He relaxed and his breathing softened. It was a gentle and tender moment.

People die differently. It is true that some will hold on until a loved one arrives to be with them. However, it is also true that some will wait until a person leaves before they die. If their family is sitting around the bed looking on, the person about to die may feel embarrassed. He may feel that he is letting people down by dying and that he would prefer not to be the focus of attention. Right up until the last moment, people are making consciously willed choices about how they would like to die.

A dying parent will sometimes prefer that their grown-up off-spring go to work rather than stay with them all day at the hospital. It will give them something to talk about in the evening. People dying run out of things to say and sometimes read the newspapers to know what to talk about when friends come to visit them. They will be tired and conversations can feel a strain. If everyone is waiting at the hospital, the only narrative is death. It can feel as if people are sitting and waiting for the inevitable to happen. If a family member is doing something else, there is another narrative to feed into the process. People dying don't simply want to talk about their own death. Parents want to know that their children are all right and will carry on their lives without them.

For a dying person, friends are like the labourers in the vineyard where those who have worked all day are paid no more than those who started work at the eleventh hour. There is no credit given by the person dying to someone who has been a friend for their whole life. A nurse, or someone they meet close to the end, can be their best friend in their last days. Kinship or empathy might be more welcome to someone dying than grief or despair.

Christian narrative of death

The New Testament asks that we take seriously a two-stage process of death and resurrection – first of sleeping or being with Christ (1 Thess. 4.14), and only after that of the remaking of ourselves at the end (1 Cor. 15.52–56).

Wright (2003) refers to the two-stage process as 'life after death' followed by 'life after life after death'. The latter comes with our full resurrection on the Last Day, as Jesus comes again. We will be resurrected, with our body renewed, as was Jesus. He was flesh and blood but also able to come through locked doors (Luke 24.39; John 20.19). This transformation into what Wright (2003) calls 'trans-physicality' is repeated for all believers at the second coming (1 Thess. 4.14).

There are two New Testament passages that deal specifically with the question of death and beyond:

> [It will happen] in a flash, in the twinkling of an eye, at the last trumpet. For the trumpet will sound, the dead will be raised imperishable, and we will be changed ... At the resurrection people will neither marry nor be given in marriage; they will be like the angels in heaven (1 Cor. 15.52; Matt. 22.30).

The pastoral logic of the Corinthians passage is that on the Day of the Lord we will meet again with those whom we have known and loved before. The inference of the Matthew passage is that while people will relate differently, they will be real to one another. Herein lies the good news of the faith that the Church has to offer to society.

Christianity offers a teleological view of history. This is to say that there is an order and purpose to the world that will come to fulfilment when we meet face to face with God. The heaven that we long for is made up out of the empirical social reality of which we are a part. Jesus died because it took his crucifixion followed by a physically resurrected and transformed body to overcome death and provide us with the promise of eternal life.

Death is not a tragedy. It is God's crowning mercy. It is through death that God in Christ draws us to himself and holds all things together (2 Cor. 5.19; Col. 1.15–19). Cocksworth (2008) writes that it is Christ's capacity to hold together the whole of creation that is the basis of his redemptive ministry in bringing together sinful estranged humanity (Col. 1.21) and the God of grace (Col. 1.2).

Society's narrative of death

The Anglican Common Worship says:

> From the rising of the sun to its setting, let us pray to the Lord . . .
> That all who have with Christ entered the shadow of death
> may rest in peace and rise in glory.

Changing the question from 'How will we "rise in glory"?' to 'Will I get into heaven?' privatizes and spiritualizes the gospel message rather than recognizes the corporate, social and political nature of the resurrection. We all rise together at the Second Coming of Christ.

Death is starting to have the same position in the modern life and literature that sex had in the Victorian times: we don't want to talk about it. D. H. Lawrence calls it our dirty little secret. A society that is uncomfortable with death is also uncomfortable with old age. In our society old people are patronized for being elderly rather than lionized for being senior citizens. In 2050 people over the age of 65 will represent a quarter of the population in the most developed countries against 16 per cent today.

Fewer and fewer people attend church and the cultural memory of Christianity is receding. Daniele Hervieu-Léger (2000) describes this as a process of secularization, which leaves people exposed, and without a narrative of death. For Hervieu-Léger, the Christian memory is a collective one and, without the legitimating authority of the Church to provide coherence and continuity, the memory disintegrates into a loose collection of subjective beliefs, practices and symbols that are reinterpreted according to families' personal preferences and choices.

The less the words of the funeral liturgy mean to a family, the more important becomes the act of remembering the person who has died. Funerals become bespoke rituals with the priest being the master of ceremonies managing the event. People speak warmly of the person who has died. Religion has gone away, said the novelist A. S. Byatt, and all we are left with is ourselves. Vanstone (1977) describes funerals as the very last 'me moments'.

The challenge to clergy visiting the bereaved is to offer a theological narrative of hope as well as a social script of comfort without one cancelling out the other. The former is the general resurrection of the dead when heaven and earth are joined together (2 Pet. 3.13). The latter is talked about in the context of the person who has died having gone to a better place. The tragedy is that the Christian understanding of death is lost in the telling and heaven is seen as a kind of hyper-spiritual existence up in the clouds.

The Church colludes with a social script that sees the person as having gone to a better place. Jesus did not die so that the disembodied souls of the faithful could leave their physical selves behind and float up to heaven as a reward for faithful living. The Church, like Esau (Gen. 25.34), is selling her inheritance for a mess of potage if all she has to offer to the bereaved family is spirituality. Wright (2003) says that the classic Christian answer to the question of death and beyond is not so much disbelieved, as not known. Jesus' resurrection is the beginning of God's new project not to snatch people away from earth to heaven but to colonize earth with the life of heaven. That, after all, is what the Lord's Prayer is about.

The idea of us going to heaven turns biblical teaching on its head. It is not us who go to heaven but, instead, heaven that comes to us in the person of Christ (Phil. 3.20). The Lord's Prayer talks about heaven coming down to earth, not about souls flying up to heaven. The new heaven and new earth are going to be on earth, not in the sky (Rev. 21.1). If families are told that death is a soul set free, they miss out on the physicality of the general resurrection, which is the real good news story of the Christian faith. The Church misses out on the eschatology that underpins the claims of Christ as the living God.

Pastoral sensitivity and doctrinal accuracy are not always the easiest of companions. The first time that the minister meets with the family will be to plan the funeral. I visit a woman, widowed after 50 years of marriage. She snorts with laughter when I ask her whether her husband used to snore. When I leave the house after planning her husband's funeral service, she says 'Thank you for making me laugh'. The language of laughter and tears cross over with each other. We describe ourselves as crying with laughter and shedding tears of joy. The family wants to be comforted and to be helped through the process. They do not want to have the Christian narrative of life beyond death explained to them. The Day of the Lord is a subject at the heart of our Christian faith, but one that needs to be treated with humility with a family who know nothing of, or have little interest in, the faith.

A Christian narrative of death is lost because people want the funeral of a loved one to be a celebration of their life rather than a mourning of their death. As the religious language used by previous generations fades, it loses the ability to comfort the bereaved. The traditional funeral prayer is for God to give us the wisdom and grace to use aright the time that is left to us here on earth. This has now become Monty Python's 'Always Look on the Bright Side of Life' or Frank Sinatra's 'I Did it My Way', which are popular choices for songs at funerals.

I use literature and quotes to help people to use their experience of the death of a loved one to help them to reflect on their own lives. I tell families that it is in death that we learn to appreciate the life that we have been given. In *Les Miserables*, at the end of his life, Valjean tells Cosette 'it is nothing to die. It is dreadful not to live.' 'Death is very likely the single best invention of life', said Steve Jobs in 2005, 'mortality is what helps us make the big changes in life. Time is short and we are not to waste it living someone else's life.'

I tailor a bespoke funeral service that crystallizes the issues the Church has to face in wanting to provide a coherent Christian narrative of death for a secularized society. The funeral is for Simon, aged 25, who has been killed in a motorcycle accident. There is a presentation of pictures from Simon's life going on through the service. People tell stories of Simon. One person reads out a letter, which he has written as if it were from Simon to his girlfriend. Someone drives a motorcycle slowly through the church door and up the aisle to the coffin. It is a tribute to Simon's passion for bikes. Friends set up a Facebook site where people can lodge their tributes – memorial websites are big business.

The service offers to people as much as they are able to absorb. It is a celebration of the man that Simon had been before. The service could have had the subtitle 'no regrets'. Driving a motor-cycle up the church aisle left people comforted, but provided no Christian insight into the nature of death.

Death is addressed in our society through a mélange of different beliefs. Crematoriums have 39 versions of 'Ave Maria' on their sound system. Doves are released by the graveside to help with the process of letting go of the person who has just died. Environ-mental funerals are big business. Democratization of death comes in the wake of the Church's declining role. People are free to tailor ceremonies as suits them best.

People die holding on to a combination of half-formulated beliefs about what is involved. Wanting to choose the time and place of one's death and not to be a burden to others is stoicism. Wanting one's ashes scattered in order to become a part of creation is paganism. Thinking of death as the spirit leaving the physical body behind is Hinduism. A Christian death is to come to terms with our own mortality and to make our peace with our friends and family. Dylan Thomas wanted his father to fight against death: 'do not go gently into the night; rage, rage against the dying of the light'. I will not be thus. I will want to praise God through, as St Francis called her, Sister Death.

Reflection

Cancer is the huntsman attacking people with a combination of fear, physical pain and disappointment. Using chemotherapy to knock out cancer is like using a dragon to kill a monster. Each will cause havoc but, with Ruth, only the latter terminally so. In the days before her death from cancer my beloved friend and companion Ruth texted me thus, 'I have been praying for Christian fortitude. I rest on the word as describing something long term and enduring and I wondered what was the unique quality of Christian fortitude? It is something to do with bearing it all as a positive offering to him: 'present your bodies as a living sacrifice'.

The next day Ruth sent a further text: 'think of the cultural context. I have always found very moving the ancient's view, that for a good sacrifice, at the last, the animal must consent. It happens too! My loved springer spaniel Emmie, after struggling at the vets, went quiet in my arms and let the vet give the lethal injection – obedience to the highest power?' Did Ruth's springer spaniel Emmie live out her animal version of death – once a dog and twice a puppy?

Prayer

Heavenly Father, thank you that through Jesus you give me resurrection hope in the face of death. Teach me to lead others in confronting death, being open about its ugliness, while choosing the appropriate time to point them to its defeat, by the work of your Son who is our risen Lord. Amen.

E

Easter and Eucharist

In the Easter story Jesus' identity as the Messiah is inextricably linked with his progress towards Jerusalem. He leaves his childhood home in provincial Galilee to go to the big city, the centre of power. Jesus' message needed to be spoken in the temple for it to be understood: 'I must press on today and tomorrow and the next day – for surely no prophet can die outside Jerusalem!' (Luke 13.33). The temple was the fulcrum for the old and the new order. It was from here that Jesus drove out the traders (Matt. 21.12) and it was here that Peter preached about the new world order after Pentecost (Acts 2.46).

As Jesus led the way towards Jerusalem, the disciples were astonished, while those who followed were afraid (Mark 10.32). John Inge (2003, p. 49) wrote that in both Matthew and Mark, Jesus' biography is represented by his journey from Galilee to Jerusalem: Galilee is seen as the sphere of revelation and redemption, and Jerusalem is seen as the place of rejection (though ultimately leading to resurrection).

The events of the Easter week happened in an atmosphere of social and political volatility. Without a sense of the chaos of Jerusalem, the quietness of Gethsemane and the barrenness of Golgotha, there is no feeling of progression through the events of Holy Week. The week is marked also by Jesus' gradual process of separation from those around him. After his triumphal entry into Jerusalem he left the city to go to Bethany, where he spent the night (Matt. 21.17) – no sooner had he arrived than he began to distance himself. At the Last Supper, he pulled back from the crowds to be with the disciples. In Gethsemane he left the main body of the disciples to be with Peter, James and John. At Golgotha he was alone on the cross. The fact that he was killed outside of the city walls provides us with the overriding image of his rejection.

Easter is an attitude and Christmas is an event

The task of the Church is to tell the story. Children can offer new insights into familiar themes. Sarah (aged 8½) says that she doesn't think that it was very nice of God to send his Son to be crucified. In one sentence she has put her finger on the penal substitution debate – 'Why', she is saying, 'should Jesus be punished (penalized) in the place of sinners (substitution), to satisfy the demands of God's justice?'

Being an Easter people means living out the Easter weekend in how we relate to others. I can live the rhythm of an Easter weekend in a single day. Good Friday grief comes with Sam knocking at the door. He is just out of prison. He has nowhere to stay and is sleeping rough. I sit with Sam till past midnight waiting for a caseworker to come and find him and to take him to a hospital. Easter Sunday joy comes with Sarah who has her baby in two and a half hours flat. She is not able to get to hospital in time and the child is born on the bedroom floor. With a genius for understatement, the relieved mother describes it as 'quite exciting'.

We either mourn or else we rejoice and are glad (Matt. 5.4, 12). We are hot or cold but we are never simply dull, grey or pragmatic in how we respond to people's suffering and vulnerability (Rev. 3.15–16). When we respond to pain by simply looking for a solution to suffering – with offers of help or to respond to grief with attempts at distraction – we are increasing the isolation of the person in need because we are denying the reality of what has happened to them. We are trying to protect them from crucifixion in the hope that there is a straight route to resurrection.

The bittersweet truth of Easter Day is that just as Jesus needed to die in order to live again, so also do we need to be born again to see the face of Christ. We trivialize what a person might be suffering if we tell them simply that God is in control and everything will come right in the end – 'all they have to do is trust'! Jesus had to go through the crucifixion before he experienced his resurrection, and so also might they.

Friday

On Good Friday God shows himself to the world through the eyes of a suffering man. There is nothing attractive in him (Christ) that we should desire him (Isa. 53.2). Stripped back to the bone, to the raw heart of Jesus' obedience, people are left free to respond to the salvation story in whatever way they choose, be it rejection or belief; as says the hymn – it is 'just as I am without one plea but that thy blood was shed for me'.

Suffering and weakness draw out extremes of response in people. The crowds were either shouting Hosanna or else calling for Jesus' crucifixion. People react similarly to feebleness or disability. They are kind and supportive or embarrassed and uneasy. They are rarely in between. Jesus' crucifixion frees people to be their better or worse selves.

Saturday

Easter Saturday is the only day in the liturgical year on which the Church commemorates disappointment and failure. The disciples would have had no knowledge of what would happen 24 hours later. Their situation could be no worse. Stunned by the violence that happened the day before, the disciples would have wondered about what Jesus had said to them previously. If, as he said, he was the Light of the World, why was he left isolated, despised and rejected, repudiated by the people of God whose mission he sought to fulfil? Why did he now rest dishonoured and decaying in a grave with the wicked (Isa. 53.3, 9)? Jesus' death on the cross would have seemed to his disciples to be the end of all their dreams.

Easter Saturday offers safe spaces to people who have been disappointed. Every school child who has been bullied, every person whose marriage has ended, every worker who has been laid off can take comfort from Easter Saturday. It is a day of disappointment when people can live with what has gone wrong in their lives because they know that theirs is a part of God's overarching story that will culminate in the Easter day of resurrection.

Sunday

The idea of Christ rising from the dead strains our credulity to the limit. One can appreciate C. S. Lewis's sentiments when he expressed a sympathy for Lazarus – 'to be brought back', he said, 'and have all one's dying to do again was rather hard'. The idea of life through death is the paradox at the heart of the Christian faith. 'I am not afraid of death', says Woody Allen, 'I just don't want to be there when it happens.'

The Church is charged with offering to people the story of Jesus' crucifixion, physical resurrection, and a transformed framework for engagement with the world. Resurrection is not simply comfort for the future. It is a way of understanding the world as it is now. Our Easter attitude is redemption of catastrophe, transformation through suffering, and ultimately resurrection to new life.

The Eucharist

Our common life is forward-looking, egalitarian and hospitable. These three strands are captured in the celebration of the Eucharist:

Forward-looking

Jesus' teaching tends towards attitudes rather than actions – for example, love one another, as I have loved you (John 13.34). He leaves only a few specific directions for his disciples and eucharistic participation is one: 'And he took bread, gave thanks and broke it, and gave it to them, saying, "This is my body given for you; do this in remembrance of me"' (Luke 22.19).

A parish Eucharist can fall into the trap of allowing a retrospective feel to the sacrament, focusing more on what Christ did in the past than on the eschatological future. Instead of being a marker in between Christ's ascension and return to earth, the Eucharist becomes an indicator of stability and a set world order. The fact that the Church has celebrated Holy Communion for 2,000 years is treated as more significant than the fact that we might not do so for much longer because we know neither the time nor date of Christ's return.

The Church's view of the future is shaped by her transformational relationship with what has come before. We are a
remembering people. The memory of what has happened in the
past provides us with an education for what we might expect to
happen in the future. If things have been different in the past from
how they are now, then they can be different again in the future.
The parish priest is a subversive traditionalist turning history on its
head and bringing the story of salvation into the immediate present
as a crossroads between the things of God and the things of man.

Christianity is eschatology. We are shaped as believers of Christ
by what has not yet happened. The Eucharist is anticipatory and
forward-looking. Jesus thanked God for raising Lazarus from the
dead before, not after, he came out from the tomb (John 11.41).
In the Eucharist we give thanks for something that has not yet
happened: 'Truly I tell you, I will not drink again from the fruit
of the vine until that day when I drink it new in the kingdom of
God' (Mark 14.25).

Egalitarian

The egalitarian nature of a Eucharist service comes because people
stand shoulder to shoulder with those of a different understanding as to its significance. A structured liturgy allows for diversity
in participation. The inclusive nature of the Eucharist is that
people discover its implications as much through their participation and involvement as through any rational knowledge and
propositional truth.

The participants are carried along by the words of the service.
Involvement through prayers, singing and fellowship are the
pathways to fuller knowing. An intuitive belief in the sacrament's
significance comes before a full understanding of its credal truths.
Participation in the Eucharist is an Augustinian model of knowing: 'we believe in order that we might know; for if we wanted to
know and then believe we should not be able either to know or
to believe'.

Jesus' table fellowship gives us a model of eucharistic equality.
Fernandez (2006) says that we should see the Eucharist through
the lenses of egalitarian-type meals, such as the feeding of the
5,000, which Jesus offered throughout his ministry.

The early Church ate and shared possessions together until the cracks began to appear in their early Church egalitarianism. Ananias with his wife Sapphira kept back some of the proceeds of a land sale for themselves, bringing only a portion of it to Peter, and were challenged for so doing. When Ananias heard this, he fell down and died (Acts 5.1–5).

Hospitality

We are both guests and hosts in the celebration of the Eucharist. As with Jesus and Zacchaeus, God welcomes us and in turn we welcome Christ and all others. Jesus asks Zacchaeus to come to his home. All the people see this and begin to mutter, 'He has gone to be the guest of a sinner' (Luke 19.7). Zacchaeus responds to Jesus coming to his home by giving half of his possessions to the poor, and paying back fourfold anybody he had cheated.

Communion is an act of solidarity. In the early Church the Eucharist was called an agape meal, expressing a linkage between our social behaviour and the mystery of Jesus' last days. For us to share in the Eucharist is to recognize that we are God's guests and to learn also to see our neighbours as such. Rowan Williams (2014) writes that for the short time when we gather as God's guests at God's table, the Church becomes what it is meant to be – a community of strangers who have become guests together.

Sharing together in the Eucharist holds us accountable to one another. Receiving communion in an 'unworthy manner' means that we do so while we have unresolved issues with another person or people in the Church (1 Cor. 11.26–29). We know this because Paul has previously referred to divisions within the Church. He is upset with the Christians in Corinth who keep up social and economic divisions while taking part in the celebration of the Eucharist, thus discriminating against poorer Christians. Paul talks about people getting drunk. He tells the Corinthians that if they simply want to eat and drink they should do so in their own house. It is only after this that he refers to taking communion in an 'unworthy manner'.

Being 'worthy' or 'unworthy' to take communion is not an individual question about our moral probity, but a biblical question about our community participation. No hierarchy, no dissensions and no divisions is the revolutionary call of the Eucharist. It is modern-day individualism rather than church-based communitarianism that sees this verse as meaning that those who take communion must be worthy enough, in and of themselves, to do so. Our worthiness comes from Christ, not ourselves. The Eucharist is for people sinning, stumbling, struggling and searching:

> We take the Holy Communion not because we are doing well but because we are doing badly. Not because we have arrived, but because we are confused and travelling. Not because we are right but because we are confused and wrong. Not because we are divine but because we are human. Not because we are full but because we are hungry (Williams, 2014, pp. 53–4).

The sacraments are a church-wide, God-given, life-transforming means of grace. The celebration of the Eucharist is by definition a joint activity. There is no such thing as an on-line Eucharist because communion is not an individualistic matter (Katie Stock in conversation); it is a *body* matter. This truth is bound up in the biblical symbol of the one loaf and the one cup (1 Cor. 10.17). The archetypal Eucharist in the parish is the 'Bring and Share' lunch. The Eucharist is a sacrament of sharing and not just about 'me and my salvation'; in the same way the 'Bring and Share' is not just about me and my food. They are occasions for people to gather and share together in the body of Christ.

Reflection

Working my way through the eucharistic prayer, I invite the congregation to receive the bread and wine.

One man is clearly upset. His marriage is in tatters. His wife has given him his marching orders upon the discovery of his unfaithfulness. He and I exchange glances. Inwardly, I sense a desire to walk and weep with this man as he wrestles with his difficult Easter weekend resulting from his own choices. His Good Friday despair is moving towards the grief of Holy Saturday, and so he comes to Christ as a bruised and broken man.

He remains at the front longer than anyone else. It is a grace-filled moment of prayer. He raises his head, looking at me with his expression transformed. He turns and goes back to his seat. That afternoon we have a long telephone conversation and his marriage begins the painfully slow process of recovery and resurrection.

Prayer

Lord God, thank you for your breakthrough at Easter – for Jesus' life, death and resurrection. Help me to journey with people in their stages of despair, grief and joy as Easter unfolds for each one of them.

May I lead your Easter people into the resurrection with celebration in proclaiming your Son's death until he returns. Amen.

F

Forgiveness

The whip-crack sharpness of the responsibility and the clarity of the command in the Bible to forgive leave no room for sentimentality or misunderstanding: 'For if you forgive other people when they sin against you, your heavenly Father will also forgive you. But if you do not forgive others their sins, your Father will not forgive your sins' (Matt. 6.14–15).

'I can understand forgiving someone who has made a mistake', says Dan, a recent convert in our church, 'but not someone who has behaved deliberately wrongly.' Nothing is less obvious than forgiveness (Brunner, 1934, p. 488), but at the same time nothing is more necessary. In Scripture it is not our responsibility whether the other person deserves forgiveness or not. We are still to offer it freely.

It is the person wronged who can see most clearly what needs to be done. As with Jesus on the cross, suffering brings insight: 'The responsibility for change and forgiveness lies with those who have had to bear most in the first place and may have the least inner resources for affecting reconciliation' (Pattison, 2000, p. 200).

In the Bible the promise of forgiveness runs parallel to the command to forgive:

- God doesn't count sin (Rom. 4.8).
- God 'covers' sin (Ps. 32.1).
- God puts all our sins behind his back (Isa. 38.17).
- God 'blots out' our transgressions (Isa. 43.25).
- God '[sweeps] away' our sins 'like mist' (Isa. 44.22).
- God doesn't remember our sins (Heb. 8.12).

The choice to forgive or not to forgive is ultimately a choice between life and death; it is the choice between a slow disintegration into bitterness or else a reaching out towards a new life. This is what Isaiah offers Hezekiah, king of Israel. Isaiah writes as a poet rather than as a historian. He uses words to paint extremes. There will either be peace, harmony and fulfilment, or complete destruction and chaos. He sets before Hezekiah, the king of Israel, in beautifully crafted poetic language, vivid images of the best and worst things that could happen to Jerusalem as a consequence of his actions.

If Hezekiah repents and turns to God, then all will go well. There will be no more gloom for those in distress; the people in darkness will see a great light (Isa. 9.2). The wolf will live with the lamb and the infant will play near the cobra's den (Isa. 11.6, 8). If Hezekiah does not repent then things will collapse – destruction and chaos are inevitable. The grass withers, the vegetation goes, and nothing green is left (Isa. 15.6).

There are distant echoes from my childhood that leave me familiar with ideas of sin and responsibility. My mother tells me that if I am bored, then it is my own fault. My father repeats the idea that 'life is unfair' like a mantra, wanting me not to take things for granted. My understanding of sin emerges out of this early formed recognition that things are not as they might be. The need for my own forgiveness drives my ministry.

The reason why forgiving and being forgiven is not an optional extra is because of the linkage between forgiveness and grace. God's covenant with us is to meet responsibility and repentance with grace and forgiveness. If we don't show the former, then we don't get the latter. The unforgivable sin is any sin that a person doesn't want to give up, confess, or even ask forgiveness for – and certainly doesn't want to hear any more about it from the Holy Spirit (Mark 3.28–30).

Forgiveness puts things into a new perspective. We learn not to take ourselves too seriously. There is neither reward for virtue nor punishment for sin. The first will be last and the last will be first (Matt. 19.13). In a scene from a play by Jean Anouilh, the good are densely clustered at the gate of heaven, eager to march in, sure of their reserved seats. All at once, a rumour starts spreading: 'It seems he's going to forgive those others, too!' For a minute, everybody's dumbfounded. They look at one another in disbelief, gasping and sputtering, 'After all the trouble I went through!' 'If only I'd known this – I just cannot get over it!' Exasperated, they work themselves into a fury, start cursing God, and are refused entry into heaven. That was their final judgement – love appeared and they refused to acknowledge it. They did not want a God who let everyone off. They could not accept a God who loved so foolishly.

Forgiveness in the Church

Christianity is a small-time religion. The Father knows the very hairs on our head (Luke 12.7). Forgiveness in a church lies in the minutiae of day-to-day living. We have a flare-up between two members of our Senior Citizens Film Club. He told her that she looked too young to be at the Club. He thought he was being flattering. She thought that he was saying that she was there under false pretences and took offence. We have a stand-off between two parents in the playground who had previously been friends. She told her friend the price of her new coat and the friend thought that she was showing off. One lady in the church is repeatedly annoyed when she loses her seat to boisterous baptism groups with noisy children. Another lady has her ex-husband setting up a Facebook page to complain about her behaviour. I go to ask him to take the site down. His muscles are as tight as his anger. Both of them are racked with resentment and bitterness towards each other.

We are the motley crew that makes up the local church. We are the holders of the Christian memory, re-telling and living out the story of God's forgiveness through our shared life together and at times we manage it better than others. Forgiveness in the Church is making a cohesive whole out of fragmented individuals. It is a political event between people, not just an individual's change of heart. The point of forgiveness is to change social circumstances and not simply to alter an individual's inner disposition. Forgiveness is to rectify a wrong and not simply to make people feel better about themselves.

In Scripture forgiveness is:

- A debt forgiven (Matt. 18.21–35).

- A stone not thrown (John 8.2–11).
- A hug, kiss, robe, ring, sandals and feast (Luke 15.22–24).
- Paralysis ended (Matt. 9.1–8; Mark 2.10; Luke 5.17–26).
- Illness healed (Luke 5.17–26).
- Blindness cured (Mark 4.10–12).
- Perfume, tears, kisses (Luke 7.36–50).

Forgive and forget

The phrase 'forgive and forget' is not found in the Bible. Forgiveness is not forgetting, but remembering well – otherwise we leave ourselves open to the same thing happening again. It is remembering well what has been done that then allows for forgiveness and progress. Volf (1996) writes that memory and forgiveness run closely together; to forgive is to blame but not to punish. The gift of forgiveness is to recognize a person's wrongdoing, but not to hold it against them. Genuine forgiveness must first 'exclude' before it can 'embrace'; it must name and shame the evil, and find an appropriate way of dealing with it, before reconciliation can happen. Otherwise we are just papering over the cracks.

Forgiveness is not a once-for-all experience but also an ongoing process that does not exclude anger. Anger can be a form of dignity and a feeling of self-worth against wrongs done to us. It is also righteous indignation against wrongs done against others. These emotions are all part of being human. Forgiveness does not mean feigned indifference or pretending that what has happened doesn't matter. It means acknowledging, understanding and then forgiving. It is a gradual process and not a single moment in time; it is a journey towards wholeness – what Mackintosh (1927, p. 129) calls a voyage of anguish. Nothing is less obvious than forgiveness, but at the same time nothing is more necessary.

Struggling to forgive someone is a voyage of anguish and discovery. It is like the story, told by G. K. Chesterton (2011), of the sailor who set out from the shores of Britain to look for an island in the Pacific. Shipwrecked at sea, he is saved by the sight of land and crawls ashore on a rocky deserted coastline. The hills and the trees looked strangely familiar and the sailor realized that the storm had driven him back on himself. What he had thought of as a new country was in fact his home, and he had come back to where he had started his journey. In short succession he was able to experience relief at having escaped the storm, excitement at a new country, and the comfort of home. Thus it is for us when we are genuinely able to forgive someone who has done us wrong.

Shame and guilt

Pattison (2000) suggests that we have shifted from a 'guilt' culture to a 'shame' culture. Guilt is when we feel that we have let some-one else down; we are left feeling judged. We feel that we have broken an external code of conduct or system of ethics. Shame is when we feel that we have let ourselves down; we are left feeling anxious. Watts (2001, p. 54) comments that we feel guilt about particular behaviours that we regard as transgressions, but we feel shame about our very selves. Shame is thus a much more pervasive, less differentiated emotion than guilt (2001, p. 56).

While guilty people need forgiveness, shamed people need a sense of valued self. The mistake of the Church is to see 'shame', but read 'guilt'. Pattison (2000, p. 245) writes that a system of confession and penitence fuelled by shame, but articulated as guilt, is infinitely self-perpetuating. It is unable to foster either the integration needed for shame or the forgiveness needed for sin because often it fails to address either properly.

How do we summon the courage to walk into the land of freedom through the gate of shame? How do we let go of what might be justified anger? How do we think about our being hurt in a new light and give up what might be a well-deserved right to hit back?

Guilt needs redemption and shame needs transformation. Redemption and transformation both come through the incarnation. With the original goodness of creation, the incarnation is an act of ongoing transformation. Jesus would have come to earth for fellowship, whether or not man had sinned. 'God saw that it was good' (Gen. 1.18). With the original sin of man, the incarnation has to be an act of redemption that saves us from the consequences of sin.

The theological promise is that the redeemed and transformed believers are given an invitation to participate in the ongoing work of God's revelation, which culminates in a new heaven and a new earth (Rev. 21). It is a grand promise to make for those to whom I referred earlier. My lady is still struggling with her seat being taken in church; the two older people at our Senior Citizens Film Club are still at odds with each other; the mothers in the school playground are no closer to being reconciled. Their journey from one context to the other will start with forgiveness.

Reflection

Leading by example, as one who preaches regularly about forgiveness, I approach Celia over coffee at the end of the service. I am aware of the need to say sorry and ask her to forgive me for my brusque manner after a service some weeks before. She and her husband had approached me about baptizing their baby when I was concentrating on visitors.

As people take time to greet one another, I sense my opportunity. However, several justifications come to me as to why I should not say sorry. The chief barrier is pride and it is put up every time forgiveness is required. Yet, I cannot let this come between me and God whose Son never needs forgiveness, but demonstrates it so freely to the soldiers who put him to death on the cross.

Celia and I exchange the peace and I say what I need to say. She has a broad smile of forgiveness and gives verbal reassurance of this. I am unprepared for the emotion of relief that I experience. My wrongdoing is acknowledged but it is not held against me.

Prayer

Lord God, thank you for showing us that the horror of the cross establishes the joy of your forgiveness. Help us as we choose to forgive, and bless us with the courage we need to ask for forgiveness. Amen.

G

Grumbles and disagreements

Conflict lies at the heart of the Christian faith. Even in families, a son will turn against his father and a daughter against her mother (Matt. 10.35). Jesus did not receive any plaudits for his ministry but was sentenced to death. He came to bring not peace, but a sword that would draw out the poison from people's hearts and open the possibility of redemption and new life (Matt. 10.34).

Jesus did not look for confrontation but was clear about the inevitability of conflict. He taught his disciples to be ready to shake the dust off their feet when they felt that a conversation could no longer be continued (Matt. 10.24). He is asked by what authority he had cleared the temple of moneychangers (Matt. 21.23–32). His reply was not immediately confrontational. It went through three stages:

1 He accepted the right of the Jewish leaders to challenge him. He began a dialogue by asking them a question in return – 'John's baptism – where did it come from? Was it from heaven, or of human origin?'
2 He challenged their response to him. They claimed the right not to reply to his question and so neither would he to theirs.
3 He disagreed with their conclusion. He told them that the tax collectors and prostitutes would enter the kingdom of God before them (Matt. 21.31).

Power protects itself. The power structure that the Jewish leaders were defending would never absorb what Jesus was saying, and so would need to destroy him for its own protection. Some of Paulo Freire's (1970) key ideas about justice come from Jesus' engagement with authority. Freire writes that it is only power that springs from the weakness that will be sufficiently strong to free both oppressor and oppressed.

The crucifixion is the ultimate story of conflict resolution. It was the intelligence of the victim that made reconciliation between man and God possible. Once the Jewish authorities had made their position clear, resolution would be the coming of the Holy Spirit. For this to happen, Jesus had to die. He says to his disciples: 'It is for your good that I am going away. Unless I go away, the Advocate will not come to you; but if I go, I will send him to you' (John 16.7).

Whipped and stripped and tied to a cross, Jesus would have recognized how completely his childhood faith would be changed with the coming of the Holy Spirit. Salvation comes from the weak to the strong. The wolf might intend harm to the lamb but never the lamb to the wolf. Lesslie Newbigin (1986) wrote that a person who wields power cannot see truth; that is the privilege of the powerless. It is the person wronged who is able most clearly to see what needs to be done to resolve an issue.

Disagreements in the early Church

In the early Church disagreements helped to shape the developing orthodoxy of the fledgling Christian belief. People understand themselves more fully by reading themselves in the eyes of someone with whom they disagree: would Paul have ever fully expressed the panoramic sweep of the doctrine of justification by faith had he not appreciated the danger to the faith offered by leaders wanting Gentile converts to be circumcised?

The stand-off in Galatia between Paul and Peter was an open conflict between the two prominent leaders of the early Church (Gal. 2.11–16). The issue was whether or not Gentile converts to Christianity would need to be circumcised. What is required for salvation/justification? The early Church was at a crossroads – would Gentile and Jewish Christians be united or divided? Paul's opposition to Peter was both to his face (Gal. 2.11) and in front of everyone (Gal. 2.14). Paul was angry: 'As for those agitators, I wish they would go the whole way and emasculate themselves!' (Gal. 5.12). It was the kind of confrontation needed to mark out the significance of the issues being addressed and to bed in the centrality of justification by faith as a non-negotiable doctrine for the Church.

Would Augustine have had such a sovereign view of grace had not Pelagius denied the doctrine of original sin? The gospel of grace is inextricably bound up with the need for universal salvation. The universality of people's need for salvation is rooted in the fact of original sin from which they need to be saved. Deny the former, as did Pelagius, and there is no need to worry about the latter. Disagreement with Pelagius helped to mark out Augustine's doctrine of grace.

The Nicene creed might never have been developed had the Church not needed to defend herself against the teachings of Arius. Arianism taught that the Son was subordinate to the Father; the Son of God did not always exist, but was created by God the Father. The Council of Nicaea countered this by establishing the Trinity as the basis of Christian belief and by writing the Nicene Creed still used in the Church today.

Disagreement in the parish

It is not unusual for people to grumble about the vicar. One could easily assume that disagreements mean that things are going wrong, but they can just as easily mean that things are going right. They are an indication that people care about what is going on – the greater people's hope and the more that they have invested in a situation, the stronger will be their subsequent disappointment if things don't work out as they had envisaged. A healthy disagreement means that a relationship is in place, issues are being addressed, and resolution is possible.

The responsibility for the clergy is to take on the role of a peacemaker. The golden rule of any disagreement is to let the other person have their say. Everyone should be quick to listen, slow to speak and slow to become angry (James 1.19). We are neither to hit back (Rom. 12.17) nor to judge other people's behaviour (Matt. 7.1). I admire a lady who told me on Thursday at the PCC that we could never be friends because she did not like me, but had come towards me on Sunday to share the peace in our communion service.

Grumbles that are left to fester are different from complaints that give opportunity for issues to be dealt with constructively. The latter are an integral part of church growth. We enlarge our thinking by letting the voices and perspectives of others, especially those with whom we may be in disagreement, resonate within ourselves.

Regan (2002) describes the Church as a learning community. Disagreements are points at which this becomes especially so. A church leader learns to respond rather than to react. The former is careful and considered; the latter is more instinctive. We talk of making a response but having a reaction. A church leader takes on the role of educator, enabling people to learn from one another. Dewey (1933) describes a shared dilemma needing to be resolved as a 'forked road situation'. It requires of us that we critically reflect on our situation and then act by observing, analysing, and then selecting a route on which we will all learn and grow together.

I have a regular diet of PCC and other church committee meetings. There is a sliding scale of interaction, which goes from conversation to discussion, from discussion to disagreement, and from disagreement to argument. Disagreements are evidence of a healthy community where people are willing to work through their differences. When a disagreement becomes an argument then the opportunity for learning together is lost. Disagreements are interactional and respectful and focus on what needs to be done. Arguments hit out at the people involved. They are aggressive and judgmental. Freire (1970) describes constructive disagreement as opportunities for dialogue. The issues need to be addressed and are there to be learnt from. Dialogue, according to Freire, hinges on several things: one of them is love. Commitment arises out of love and dialogue out of commitment.

The comprehensiveness of Anglicanism with irresistibly distinct theologies alive within the same ecclesiastical communion encourages a harmonization of differences. This frustrates those who would prefer to see a greater clarity of belief, such as the discussion (on both sides) and debate on same-sex marriage.

L'Arche communities work with a flat management structure based on the principle of equality. This creates a context for healthy disagreement where each can learn from the other. A hierarchical parish structure is less comfortable with disagreement when decisions are seen as the responsibility of the leadership and the vicar feels criticized if his judgement is brought into question: 'Communities need tensions if they are to grow and deepen. Tensions come from conflicts . . . A tension or difficulty can signal the approach of a new grace of God. But it has to be looked at wisely and humanly' (Vanier, 1989, pp. 120–1).

The legacy of the *Mission-Shaped Church* (2004) debate does not lie solely in the new initiatives themselves, but also in the way that the landscape for church life has changed – the days are gone of parishes being individual fiefdoms where everything is dependent on, or decided by, the vicar. Finances have also played their part in flattening out the lay and ordained leadership structure in local churches. The wider Church is no longer able to guarantee individual congregations their own parish priest. Rural clergy might now have between four and ten parishes to contend with. Parish management has had to learn by default to be more lay-inclusive. This makes partnership a key skill for clergy – partnerships within their own congregation, with different types of church, and also with voluntary sector organizations.

Reflection

Gabriel is an energetic young Christian, gifted with people, who I know from my previous parish 20 minutes' away. He is pondering a call to ordination and needs a year to gain experience in a new setting. I am sure that I can offer him a placement in the parish. I ask the PCC if I can take him on and develop a role for him.

However, the meeting of godly people decides that there must first be a perception of need for Gabriel's particular skills and a relevant job description. We are at odds but I accept this wisdom, hiding my sense of discontent.

Within a year I hear stories of other parishes, that have to face difficult staffing issues resulting from employees without portfolios. I am grateful as I realize that my viewpoint has blanks requiring to be filled in by the contrasting outlook of others with whom God surrounds me.

Prayer

Living Lord God, thank you for the beauty of people with their differing ideas and varied opinions. You created us all uniquely and I celebrate the potential for growth through one another's different outlooks. Thank you that I can sense your Holy Spirit renewing me as I listen and as I determine which criticisms to deflect, defend or which to absorb. Help me through any period of criticism to develop myself as your disciple and leader in your Church. Amen.

H

Hospitality

There are three types of hospitality practised in the parish, each of which is the engine room to a different type of church growth. There is a 'subversive hospitality', which is when we invite those who will not invite us back. This leads to social action in the community. There is 'story hospitality', when we invite people to become a part of God's ongoing story in the world. This is evangelism and leads to an increase in the congregation as people are invited to commit their lives to Christ. There is 'fellowship hospitality' as people are invited into one another's homes. This produces an increased congregational depth through strengthening relationships and a maturity of discipleship.

1 Subversive hospitality

The parable of the great banquet (Luke 14.15–24) is an act of hospitality that overturns social structures. The original invitees quote the facts of their social inclusion as reasons for refusing the master's invitation. The fact of wealth (a new field), employment (five yoke of oxen) and prosperity (a new marriage) (Luke 14.18–20) are considered reasons enough for refusing the invitation. The ethical and political imperative of the story is for the second tranche of invitations to go to the socially excluded. These are the poor, the crippled, the blind and the lame.

Jesus' notion of hospitality continues the stream of social subversion. Dinner parties are not networking opportunities, but a chance to invite those not in a position to invite you back. Once you have committed yourself to relationships with people who do not reflect back to you, your own worldview is admitting to a wider set of concerns than simply your own:

When you give a luncheon or dinner, do not invite your friends, your brothers or sisters, your relatives, or your rich neighbours; if you do, they may invite you back and so you will be repaid. But when you give a banquet, invite the poor, the crippled, the lame, the blind, and you will be blessed. Although they cannot repay you, you will be repaid at the resurrection of the righteous (Luke 14.12–14).

We answer this by setting up a cinema club for homeless people. When asked for money by someone who is homeless, 120 congregation members now have the opportunity to build a relationship not based on the dictate of the market place or the requirements of the state. Instead of giving (or not giving) money, they can invite the individual to the cinema club where they will meet and be met on a basis of equality. One person's opinion on a film is as valid as another's. Nouwen (1975) said that hospitality is not to change people, but to offer them space where change can take place. He describes hospitality as the creation of free space where the stranger can enter and become a friend instead of an enemy.

The 2016 Brexit vote raised questions that the parish church is well equipped to answer: who is my neighbour and what claim does he or she have upon me? Reconciliation and integration of different groups within society is the Church's specialism. The Greek word for 'hospitality' is *philoxenia*: literally, 'the love of strangers'. It is the exact opposite of xenophobia, the fear of strangers.

The question of how to learn from people who are different from us shapes the Church's desire to include more black and ethnic minorities in their leadership structure. The fact, as Paul writes in Galatians (3.28), that there is neither Jew nor Gentile, neither slave nor free, nor is there male and female, for all are one in Christ Jesus, does not mean that all are of the same social and economic circumstances.

Paul's argument is not that the natural racial, gender or generational barriers and distinctions all go away, because they do not. Instead, he is saying that with a unity in Christ divisiveness becomes distinctiveness where each can learn from the other. For this to be so we recognize and rejoice in the differences between each of us and the Church becomes the welcoming and hospitable place needed by a disjointed and fragmented society.

Foucault writes about how society needs to describe certain behaviour as 'madness' in order to establish its own notions of conventionality. Extreme religion becomes that 'madness' and serves to reinforce society's view of itself as liberal and tolerant. The radicalized Islamic figure is seen as an inexpressible hostile 'other' against whom society can define itself. In the aftermath of the Brexit vote, UK nationalists hit out at Muslims to express their own dissatisfaction at the social order in which they felt increasingly marginalized. There were two categories of 'Project Fear' in the Brexit debate: one side focused on the economy, and the other on immigration. The Referendum opened up a Pandora's box of resentment and suspicion. The resentment is not going to be faced by politicians in Westminster, but in communities across the country. It will be more likely to threaten a granddad heading home after Friday prayers or a Romanian mum caught on the bus speaking her mother tongue. It is here that the parish church, for whom relationships are a speciality, comes into her own in being able to promote the well-being of the local community.

2 Story hospitality

The Church is host and guest within society. She is invitation giving – 'Come to me, all of you who are weary and burdened, and I will give you rest' (Matt. 11.28). She is invitation led – 'Anyone who welcomes you welcomes me, and anyone who welcomes me welcomes the one who sent me' (Matt. 10.40). In the Church we learn to be both astonished in the world and yet at home within it. We are in the world but not of the world (John 17.14–15).

The local church offers the hospitality of God through the story of Christ. The congregation is host to its telling. Stories are inclusive and including. The weekly gathering is an invitation to people to read themselves into the Christian story and to reimagine their lives as they might be. The biblical narratives and the Church's practices shape a distinctively Christian way of looking at the world.

In Scripture there is nothing rated worse than inhospitality. If people don't show welcome to the apostles it will be worse for them than it will be for 'Sodom and Gomorrah on the day of judgment' (Matt. 10.15). Christ appears to make our eternal fate dependent on our hospitality to those who are hungry or thirsty or a stranger (Matt. 25.34–35).

Hospitality runs through Scripture and keeps the story moving. Abraham had 318 trained servants but still he and Sarah prepare themselves the finest bread, a choice calf and some curds and milk to offer three strangers by the great trees of Mamre (Gen. 18). In Hebrew it says: 'Do not forget to show hospitality to strangers, for by so doing some people have shown hospitality to angels without knowing it' (Heb. 13.2).

There were three occasions when the disciples recognized the resurrected Jesus through food. On the shores of the Lake of Genesaret Jesus greeted the disciples with a breakfast of bread and fish (John 21.9). It was in the physical act of eating together that the disciples recognized Jesus. On the road to Emmaus they only realized who Jesus was when they sat down to eat together (Luke 24.31). Jesus the guest became Jesus the host through the breaking of the bread. In Jerusalem the disciples fed Jesus with broiled fish (Luke 24.41b–43).

3 Fellowship hospitality

Hospitality is embedded within the DNA of a parish. The traditional role of the clergy is to give and to receive hospitality. They will visit people in their homes and invite them to their own. The working assumption is that the clergy house will be used for hospitality. Clergy make a virtue out of living on the job. They claim garden maintenance and domestic expenditure back from the taxman because these are seen as legitimate employment costs.

Clergy can grow defensive if they feel a pressure from the parish to entertain. They may feel that they have children to protect, or a working partner to support. They may simply be living in a modern vicarage that does not lend itself to hospitality. This privatization of space simply reflects society's values back on to itself and throws the question of hospitality back on to the parish church; if the meals are not taking place in the vicarage then they need to happen elsewhere.

The ultimate call of hospitality is that we need others to be ourselves. Richard (2000) writes that hospitality requires attentive listening and a willingness to enter into another's world and be transformed. The welcome of hospitality, he argues, performs the transformation of oneself by the existence of the 'other'.

In the Old Testament the integrity of Israel is dependent on its treatment of the stranger in its midst (Zech. 7.9–10). In the New Testament it is our neighbour who enables us to become the people that we have it within us to be; we are told to love our neighbours as ourselves (Mark 12.31).

Pipkin is a rabbit in Richard Adams's book *Watership Down*. Though weak and in constant need of help, Pipkin plays the most significant role in shaping the character of the rabbit warren. By endangering themselves to care for Pipkin, the other rabbits develop an ability to be open to the stranger. Pipkin's gift to the community was to allow them to be their most generous selves by his ability to accept their gifts without feeling that he owed them anything in return.

In our church Kumar was our Pipkin. For two years he was a part of our congregation and embodied for us the conundrum of the illegal immigrant. Legally and socially he was pulled towards the edges of society. He worked late at night in restaurant kitchens, but was eventually deported. Theologically he was drawn into the centre of the church community where, in offering him our hospitality, we learnt to be our better selves.

We learn about ourselves

Jesus changed water into wine at a wedding reception at the start of his public ministry. Three years later the Church began with a meal. Once Pentecost was finished the believers gathered in their homes and ate together with glad and sincere hearts (Acts 2.46). Tea and coffee after church is our tame modern-day equivalent.

I decide to follow the example of the early Church. I invite everyone on our church's electoral role of 120 to dinner. There is a natural momentum to the idea. Evenings are out of the ordinary for people and are fun. People like the idea of being invited to the vicarage. Do vicars really drink sherry? There is an abiding cultural fascination with how the clergy eat their food – 'More tea, Vicar?' or 'Would you prefer a little sherry with your mince pies?'

Over this period of eating together the meals shape the church organically through the relationships built between the people who gather together. They shape the church missionally through my exampling hospitality and encouraging people to do the same with others. Hospitality is the responsibility of all. Abraham and Sarah had 318 servants, yet still he and Sarah prepare food themselves for the three strangers (Gen. 18).

The meals shape the church prophetically through putting together people of different ages, racial, cultural and friendship groups who have grown used to sitting near to one another in church but have not yet had a conversation. There are people who have been going to church for a number of years, have sat a few rows apart, but do not yet know one another's names.

Hospitality offers people the chance to feel a part of, and to belong to, a wider community. Simone Weil was a French female mystic, who died in 1943 at the age of 34. Despite a long practice of self-starvation, she wrote that 'to be rooted is perhaps the most important and the least recognized need of the human soul ... People are rooted by virtue of a real active and natural participation in the life of a community.'

Reflection

As Easter approaches, the church puts on a Passover meal, drawing all types of people from every corner of the parish. There is a generous budget for all the lamb, which is enjoyed by everyone, many of whom cannot afford to buy such meat for themselves. I am thrilled to be able to offer hospitality to people in the church and community.

As we start the meal the liturgy takes over, and I invite people to say together the words that chart God's salvation history through the Old Testament and into the New Testament. This culminates in a chorus of acknowledgements from all of us of the sacrifice of the Lamb on the cross. Andrew, who has not been in a church for years, tells me this experience is bringing him back to God. He mingles with others enjoying fellowship after a long time away.

Prayer

Heavenly Father, we thank you that you transform us by your hospitality. May we be hosts to others and demonstrate your kindness, as we stand at the foot of the cross, ready to welcome others to join the story. Amen.

I

Identity

Identity in Christ

The Church is a still-point in a moment of time offering a glimpse into eternity. It is tranquil, familiar and comforting. Hymns that punctuate the silence and prayers that plead to God on behalf of the whole world offer a reassuring cradle of significance set against the backdrop of eternity: 'But the fruit of the Spirit is love, joy, peace, forbearance, kindness, goodness, faithfulness' (Gal. 5.22).

Parish theology is a re-creation, not simply a recollection of God's ways in the world. I am able to spend time with a Muslim convert to Christianity. He is not even aware that Matthew is the name of one of the Gospels, nor that the Bible is divided into the Old and New Testaments. As we meet together, read the Bible and pray, he is not simply learning the Christian narrative but becoming a part of the story himself.

Our identity in Christ comes through being immersed in Scripture

> I pray that the eyes of your heart may be enlightened in order that you may know the hope to which he has called you, the riches of his glorious inheritance in his holy people (Eph. 1.18)

We root our identity in Christ by learning to see through the eyes of our heart and re-imagining our lives through the range of incidents, depth of teaching and range of characters in Scripture. We enter the salvation narrative. We are Adam and Eve once more, naked and afraid, hiding from God and putting on garments of animal skin to cover our shame from one another. Eating the apple was the symptom – not the cause of – what was wrong. Adam's sin was apathy, taking for granted what he had and failing to appreciate the goodness and love of God.

If Jesus were to return to earth today people would be equally lethargic. Society would not crucify him. It would trivialize him by making him an object of media interest. Jesus would feature on the *News at Ten*, appear on chat shows, and be blogged about on the internet. Then, when our interest had waned, the press would focus its attention elsewhere. It would be death by indifference rather than by killing. We would not need to reject the truth because we would not have taken it seriously enough in the first place. We miss the central point of the Christian story. The radical nature of evil, the reality of death and our fear of nothingness have all been overcome by the love of God.

Identity in Christ comes through being a part of a Christian community

The revolutionary call of a local church is to have people commit themselves to healing existing broken relationships and making new relationships in the name of Christ. A key task for the church minister is to build up a distinctive and holy community of belief and lead it as it shapes out the reality of God's love in the world. The church is not simply a community of shared interest where like-minded people gather together.

A Christ-centred and outward-looking church draws in people who might otherwise never have met or spent time together. A vital contribution that the church makes to a new social order is to be a new social order herself: 'Corporate worship, alongside those who are different, is essential for spiritual growth; the relaxed and congenial experience of eating, talking and maybe praying with friends is not enough to sustain discipleship in post Christendom' (Murray, 2004, p. 210).

The gospel is about God's purpose to unite all things in Christ. This is crystallized at the point in the Eucharist where the congregation shares the 'peace of Christ' one with another. In Scripture the claims of discipleship are given greater prominence than the kinship of family (Mark 3.34). Sharing the peace with a stranger invites us to have that level of claim upon each other. This realignment of relationships is politics, not simply feelings, because it is creating a new community. It acts out the promise of eschatology when all are drawn together in one. We imagine how we would behave differently towards the other person if the Kingdom of God were already present, and then we realize that in so doing the Kingdom already is.

A parish church that is able to draw together people from across the local area becomes a microcosm of the community in which it is placed. Churches embody a particular tradition of practice and vision of the world. Local churches are well placed to identify the common good of the communities in which they are located. A parish church is a community for the sake of others. The church is a community among other communities.

It is back-to-front thinking to see our primary task as getting more people into church rather than building a community of people capable of witnessing to God's truth in the world. If we do the latter, then the former will happen automatically. If we attempt the former first then we will see the church is 'seduced into irrelevance trying to change things outside of itself in a society that could not care less about Jesus' (Tomlin, 2009).

Identity in Christ comes through challenging social assumptions

Our identity in Christ is more often threatened by lethargy or indifference rather than hostility or persecution. A challenge for the Church is to challenge others; to keep our minds clear for what is needed for a life of faith in Christ. Seeing the face of Christ in the poor, dispossessed and transient is upside-down thinking in a society that puts a premium on ability, wealth and social connections.

To have our identity rooted in Christ we need the weapon of ideas to challenge lazy social assumptions over what makes for a well-lived life. A job of the Church is to avoid clutter and to keep our minds clear for Christ. The Church embraces:

- Hope rather than optimism. Optimism is positive thinking (always look on the bright side of life). Hope is faith in the risen Lord.

- Joy rather than simply happiness. Happiness is circumstantial (originating from the Latin word *hap*, meaning chance). Joy is a character-based attitude to life. A person might be happy at one moment but unhappy in another. The point is to be able to rejoice in the Lord always (Phil. 4.4).

- Love rather than simply tolerance. Love is infinitely more than tolerance. To tolerate one another suggests separateness and a clinical accommodation, and leaving one another alone is precisely what Christians cannot do. The love of God that we are asked to copy is a wholehearted commitment to the well-being of others. It is not the clinical detachment of tolerance.

- Scepticism rather than cynicism. A sceptic is someone who doesn't believe anything without strong reasons. There is every reason for a Christian to be sceptical. We set our minds on things above, not on earthly things, and hence we are one step removed from any immediate acceptance of everything we are told (Col. 3.2). A cynic believes the worst in people. To be cynical is to distrust other people's motives. It is an attitude characterized by an absence of faith or hope. There is no place for cynicism in the life of faith.

Identity in Christ is the way of the cross (Matt. 16.24–25)

Sometimes the way of the cross is an inability to help ourselves. A friend's death from cancer is just such a situation. It takes the best of who I am and uses it against myself because in helping another to share in her last moments, I script myself out of the narrative of events surrounding her death. I spend the days leading up to her death caring for others, talking with the undertakers, and arranging the funeral service. I make the arrangements for her funeral so that others will not need to.

My public role as a priest denies me my personal needs as a friend. I am like Peter the disciple, caught by his own good motives, reaching out beyond himself and then learning from his own discomfort. The Christian virtues of charity and service (1 Cor. 13; 1 Peter 4.10) take away what I need for myself and gives it to others.

The time bomb that my dear friend's death leaves me with is recognition that I will sometimes need more from situations than the formal religious structures of priesthood allow. If I am constantly looking to the needs of others, then I risk creating a life in which I have no part. Bonhoeffer wrote that 'when Christ calls a man, He bids him come and die'. I am left wondering whether I am strong enough for this challenge.

Sometimes the way of the cross is an inability to help others. I am sitting with a homeless person. People who live on the streets have a life expectancy (47) of 30 years less than the general population and rough sleeping has risen nationally by 37 per cent since 2010. It is not uncommon for a person to be released from prison with nowhere to live. Prisoners and ex-offenders are treated as intentionally homeless if it is due to rent arrears resulting from their time in prison.

Sam is in this position. He lies huddled up in his sleeping bag outside the church, hoping that a homelessness caseworker will find him before the police come and move him on. He is freshly out of prison. I have rung round to try to get him a bed for the night. I sit with him until midnight. Neither caseworker nor police appear.

In the morning he has gone. It is a few days before I find out what has happened to him. I receive a letter. He was picked up by the police and was back in prison 24 hours after leaving. He wrote to me from the prison, thanking me for spending time with him. We learn about God through our relationships with the poor and dispossessed. The glory of God in Isaiah (42.3) is a bruised reed.

Reflection

I go to my bedroom and open the Bible. I have a struggle between my desire to serve God in the way in which I want, and that which seems most possible at the moment. I want to carve out my own path according to what brings me delight and a desire to advance. Yet there is a check in my spirit. I have an hour and I use it to read through Ecclesiastes. It speaks reassuringly into my feelings of indecision: 'Whether a tree falls to the south or to the north, in the place where it falls, there it will lie' (Eccles. 11.3). Initially this half-verse seems ridiculously obvious. Yet I dwell on it and the words go in. I realize that I am still willing the tree that is my life to fall the way I want it to go. This is a moment of triumph and a significant weight lifts off my spirit. I am encouraged to know that my identity is affirmed once again as one for whom the tree has fallen the way God intended and I am serving Christ according to the Holy Spirit's calling. Pushing the tree a different way may be what I want for now, but it is not going to succeed. All is in God's time and for his glory alone.

Prayer

Heavenly Father, I thank you for my identity in your Son, our Lord Jesus Christ. As I lead others in re-creating your ways in the world, help me to read Scripture so that my roots in him go deep. Let me worship with those who are both like me and not like me. Let me follow my Saviour's example in being an upside-down thinker in the face of the world's quest for prestige or possessions. I want to lose my life for his sake and so to walk humbly in the way of the cross. Amen.

J

Joy

Joy in the Bible

Jesus explodes conventional linguistic categories as he outlines the joyful new reality of the kingdom of heaven on earth. He is quick with one-liners, such as, 'Let the dead bury their dead' (Matt. 8.22). He conjures up memorable images, comparing fault-finding to a big piece of wood in someone's eye (Matt. 7.3). He nicknames Peter (the man who is to deny him) as the 'Rock' and James and John as 'Sons of Thunder'. He lists a series of scenarios, none of which are ever likely to happen. Whoever is likely to cook without salt, put a light under a bushel, cast pearls before swine, put new wine in old wineskins, give scorpions to their children or build a tower without seeing whether he has enough money to afford it? (Matt. 5.13, 5.15, 7.6, 9.17; Luke 11.11, 14.28).

Mark tells the gospel story with high tempo energy. The word *euthus* (immediately) occurs 42 times in Mark alone. The Spirit immediately drove him out into the wilderness (Mark 1.12): 'At once they [the disciples] left their nets and followed him' (Mark 1.18). The days in Galilee are shot through with amazement. Crowds follow him (Mark 8.34); he raises people from the dead (Mark 5.41). He heals the sick and drives out demons (Mark 3.7–12).

Joy is the reason for this brief fast-paced telling of the gospel story. The angels start with joy (Luke 2.10); the disciples end with joy (Luke 24.52); Jesus pursues joy (Heb. 12.2). G. K. Chesterton wrote that man is more himself, man is more manlike, when joy is the fundamental thing in him and grief the superficial. Jesus never concealed his tears and he never restrained his anger. Yet:

There was in that shattering personality a thread that must be called shyness. There was something that He hid from all men when He went up the mountain to pray. There was something that He covered constantly by abrupt silence or impetuous isolation. There was some one thing that was too great for God to show us when He walked upon the earth; and I have sometimes fancied that it was His mirth (Chesterton, 2011, p. 184).

Joy in the parish

The joy of being a church leader is to see the world through other people's eyes. The skill is that of an intuitive accompanier. I find myself scripted in to whatever is important to the other person at the time. I am chaplain to the local football club and a player asks me if I have any tattoos on my body. He shows me some of his own. I am a volunteer at a weekly meal for the homeless. A homeless person thinks that I want clothes for myself. He shows me the best of those that are being distributed. I help to run a parent and toddler group. A mother tells me how she was not allowed to take her breast milk on to a plane because she had it stored in a container that was too big for airport regulations. I am whoever people want me to be. For the sake of the gospel, that I might share in its blessings I have become all things to all people (1 Cor. 9.19–23).

Joy is commanded in the Bible because joy is an invitation for us to imitate God. Joy, like God, wants nothing more than to be itself and to include others in the process. Parish joy is poignant and slapstick. I start one Sunday dressed as a donkey crawling round the church with children trailing after me as a part of our All Age Service. On Monday morning I am at our parent and toddler group and singing 'If I were a butterfly' (for the umpteenth time).

A joyful parish church is fabulous and fragile. A church congregation combines the tenuousness of new relationships with the loyalty of the long-standing members and the hope expressed through people coming together and greeting each other in the name of Christ. There is nothing on earth so transforming as a Church in love. Everything that happens, everything that is said and done and thought and felt, is reducible to one question and that is: what can be taught or learnt about God? This must involve passion, excitement and feeling: 'For the kingdom of God is not a matter of eating and drinking, but of righteousness, peace and joy in the Holy Spirit' (Rom. 14.17).

Generating joy

I find a quiet joy in the silence in the few moments immediately after I have prayed with another, before either of us begins to talk. Joyful people worry less. Worry is me-centred rather than God-focused (Matt. 6.25). People who worry end up like Eeyore wondering whether the sky was going to fall on his head. 'It's snowing still,' said Eeyore gloomily. 'So it is.' 'And freezing.' 'Is it?' 'Yes,' said Eeyore. 'However,' he said, brightening up a little, 'we haven't had an earthquake lately.'

Joy is a fruit rather than a gift of the Holy Spirit and therefore needs to be worked at (Gal. 5.22). Just as much as we are commanded to keep the Sabbath, we are commanded to rejoice (Phil. 4.4). To rejoice is a choice. If there are plants growing in the church guttering and the roof needs attention, to rejoice always, pray continually and give thanks in all circumstances is a discipline rather than an instinct (1 Thess. 5.16–18).

Being joyful is a conscious decision and not a circumstantial happiness. I am in a New Year's Service in India. On the stroke of midnight, the church door slams open. A wizened stick-thin rubbish collector, with his back bent due to the weight of the sack that he is carrying, enters the church. People like him are a familiar sight. They are desperately poor and gather rubbish from the street for the chance to earn a few rupees. The congregation is perturbed and wonders what he is going to do. He walks to the front of the church and puts his rubbish bag down in front of the altar. He thanks God loudly for the year he has just had and then leaves the church.

Joy looks beyond the immediate happenings of day-to-day life. Glimpses of eternity are the heart of a church leader's vocation. On one occasion I have the family of a lady in hospital contact me. Seventeen years previously while serving my curacy in a different parish, she had made me promise that I would be there

when her 'time comes'. Now she is in hospital getting ready to die
and she wants me to come. I go to pray with her and she tells me
that she can see a vision of angels. It is the unpredictable, untidy,
unencumbered nature of grace from a powerful, playful and
intriguing God that underpins the work that I do in the parish. I
dance the unfettered rhythms of grace.

Joy is contagious and participative. It draws people in to a
shared communal process of worship and fellowship. In the joy of
others lies our identity as Christ's new creation (2 Cor. 5.17). A
young person who has grown used to being treated with suspicion
by adults that he meets, finds in church a different version of himself reflected in the joyful eyes of others.

Joy is also an act of subversion against a consumer culture
because it is self-sufficient and all-encompassing. Joyful people
have no need to be covetous, greedy or possessive because they
are delighted with what they have already. There is none of the
desire for more, upon which consumerism so heavily relies. Joy is
an alternative to the strivings of an aspirational society because
joyful people are happy as they are. Joy is an antidote to the atomized and segregated society in which we live because joyful people
forge their sense of identity by being with other people.

Worship is a form of play and playing is how we act out our joy
in Christ. As we sing hymns and choruses we imagine the world
differently from how it is. Animals play to practise the skills they
will need later on in life. Children play in order to experiment
with different ways of being in their world. Adults 'play' together
in church, believing that the world can be different to how it now
is:

God is working his purpose out
as year succeeds to year:
God is working his purpose out,
and the time is drawing near;
nearer and nearer draws the time,
the time that shall surely be,
when the earth shall be filled
with the glory of God
as the waters cover the sea.

'Playing in Christ' comes from being a part of the skittish, flexible, playful, experimental nature of the Holy Spirit. Genuine free-spirited playfulness takes energy, concentration and whole-heartedness and there has to be someone either to play with or against. This is the Holy Spirit, the connector, the transformer and the maker of relationships.

Reflection

Towards the end of one Sunday morning service, I am standing at the front of the church waiting to receive the offering while the penultimate hymn is being sung. I can feel myself stressed from the pressure of getting everything in the service done correctly. I am intrigued at the joy sketched across the faces of a young couple I know well. We have already been in touch that weekend about dreadful employment issues he is facing. The two of them are fearful for their future.

I glimpse their passion as they sing. It challenges and encourages me. They choose to abandon the self-absorption of their difficulties in favour of intentional praise to our Almighty God who, despite our circumstances, can be trusted to be the same – yesterday and today and for ever (Heb. 13.8). This decision draws them ever closer into the wonder and mystery of their relationship with him through Jesus. The final hymn becomes, for me, one of the most joyful I can ever remember.

Prayer

Lord, thank you for the endless possibilities of joy. I am sorry that I often struggle to be joyful. Forgive me for the times that I have been guilty of not showing joy to my congregation. Help me to go back to the basics of the joy of the resurrection – to study it, to ponder it, to discuss it, to pray it through. Make me a transparent agent of your Spirit, a bubbling stream of the living water of joy for others, flowing from the authentic, frequently rediscovered truth of the eternal hope in your Son's return. Amen.

K

Knowledge and other faiths

Foucault (2006) writes about how society needs to describe certain forms of behaviour as 'madness' in order to establish its own notions of conventionality. Extreme religion becomes that 'madness' and serves to reinforce society's view of itself. The radicalized Islamic figure is seen as an inexpressible hostile 'other' against whom society can define itself. In the aftermath of the 2016 Brexit vote, UK nationalists hit out against Muslims and other immigrants to express their own dissatisfaction at the social order in which they felt increasingly marginalized. It is here that the parish church, for whom relationships are a speciality, comes into her own in being able to promote the well-being of the local community.

The salience of religion has become more apparent over the last few years as non-Christian faiths have grown as a proportion of the population and, following 9/11, religious radicalization has challenged Western ideals. Both of these disproportionately affect young people – it is those under 30 years of age who form the most religiously diverse group; and it is young people (albeit a very small minority) who are most likely to be attracted to various forms of religious extremism. The public response to these developments has not been to become more religious, but rather to try and cater for the needs of legitimate minority religious groups as far as possible without compromising secular liberal values, and to contain those people who are perceived as dangerous.

Young people tend to echo the general societal tolerance of other people's religions so long as they do not proselytize or jeopardize a young person's own personal beliefs and values. This tolerance is commensurate with the trend towards religious privatization and an attitude of 'benign indifference' to something that does not appear to matter that much anyway (Collins-Mayo, Mayo and Nash, 2010). As far as religious orientation is concerned, young people in the main are happy to see it as a case of 'each to their own'.

The Church is wrong-footed when she finds herself set up against Islam as competitor for the truth. The two theistic worldviews have more in common with each other than a secular liberalism that denies God's existence. Islam, in one generation, can no more be thought of in terms of ISIS than can Christianity, in a previous generation, be equated with the IRA. Islam and Christianity are universal religions wanting to appeal to all.

Francis Fukuyama (1992) wrote of 1992 as the end of history. The great ideological battles between the East and West were over. Western liberal democracy had triumphed and a free market economy was the social order of the day. Religions have to take their place in a market place of ideas. Non-liberalism or intolerance towards religion has become the new social taboo in the way that single parenthood would have been in the 1950s.

People are expected to keep their religious beliefs private; hence they are thought of as fanatics when they do otherwise. Religion is seen as being entirely a matter of conscience and individual choice. When Christianity is targeted, as has happened with a nurse suspended for offering to pray for a patient (Caroline Petrie in 2009), an air stewardess for wearing a cross (Miss Eweida in 2006), or a school receptionist for talking about her faith (Jennie Cain in 2009), the Church has been able to do no more than to insist on her right to be heard, thus appealing to the same value base that has put her in that position in the first place. Evangelism is perceived as Christians giving their opinion rather than witnessing to the truth. This leaves us with a society short of sympathy for a Church short of practice in making definitive statements of belief. Religious collaboration is the order of the day.

Truth and belief

The Christian story is to turn the stranger into friend. I have the opportunity to do so with a request for her child to be baptized from a mother (Thali) who is a practising Muslim and whose father is a Christian. In the previous generation Thali's Christian mother had brought her up as a Muslim, even though her father had left the family. Now a generation later she is married to a Christian man and wants to honour what her mother had done previously by agreeing for her son to be baptized into the Christian faith. Contemporary family life has established the precedent of a single parent driving the decision for baptism, and so I concur. The family, friends and godparents who gather for the baptism are a mixture of people from both the Christian and the Islamic faith. I tell the assembled Islamic group to listen respectfully, share the occasion gladly, but not to join in when any affirmations of belief are made. They are a participative audience to the central Christian sacrament.

Our baptism service is an act of inclusion. We are drawing the Islamic family into our story in order to share in theirs. In the Old Testament the integrity of Israel is dependent on their treatment of the stranger in their midst (Zech. 7.9–10). In the New Testament we love our neighbours as ourselves (Mark 12.31). Strangers and neighbours and the relationships in between become joined together.

An inclusive approach to other faiths says that while a non-believer might not have the fullness of revelation in Christ, they will have an understanding of God's Spirit and hence things from which we can learn. God speaks to the Gentiles in nature (Rom. 1.20), in history (Acts 17.26), in reason (John 1.9) and through the conscience (Rom. 2.14–15). We look for the hidden Christ in others.

Even the Christian cannot be absolutist about their own salvation. 'Not everyone who says to me, "Lord, Lord," will enter into the kingdom of heaven' (Matt. 7.21). Salvation is not a contract between the individual and God secured by a commitment of faith. It is a relationship between God and man shaped by how we relate to the most vulnerable within society:

Then the righteous will answer him, 'Lord, when did we see you hungry and feed you, or thirsty and give you something to drink? When did we see you a stranger and invite you in, or needing clothes and clothe you? When did we see you ill or in prison and go to visit you?' The King will reply, 'Truly I tell you, whatever you did for one of the least of these brothers and sisters of mine, you did for me' (Matt. 25.37–40).

Our baptism service is an act of invitation. We are the hosts, the family are the guests, and the baptism service is our place of encounter. We are different in order to know our need of each other and therein lies our common humanity. We are people of grace who have to have the vulnerability of Jesus from the cross. The baptism will be celebrating what Desmond Tutu calls our 'glorious diversity'.

Lord Jakobovitz commented in the House of Lords (3 May 1988):

From schools that had confidence in their Christianity I learnt an answering pride in my Jewishness and I discovered that those who best appreciate other faiths are those who treasure their own. We are different in order to know our need of each other and therein lies our common humanity.

In the baptism service the parents and godparents are asked:

Do you turn to Christ as Saviour?
Do you submit to Christ as Lord?
Do you come to Christ, the way, the truth and the life?

Far from feeling disconcerted at her husband being asked, 'Do you turn to Christ?' Thali was glad at the respect we gave to our faith. Her main concern was that her husband took his baptismal vows seriously and that her child would have a God-centred upbringing.

Many cultures rather than multicultural

The raison d'etre of the Church is to bring people together and this is helping to mark the end of an extended period where cultural norms have kept people separated in the name of multi-culturalism. The demarcation of urban areas along racial lines first emerged during the postwar years. Many Asian and black immigrants were housed in slum areas, such as the East End of London, after the white working class had evacuated them into the suburbs. Allocating social housing along racial lines, and in the process creating 'ghettos', continued to be official policy of local authorities throughout the 1980s and 1990s. Such allocations were institutionally justified via the language of multiculturalism and diversity. Rather than the allocation of resources being categorized on basic economic need, local authorities stress the importance of recognizing the cultural 'differences' of racial groups.

Tolerance is not a statement of open-mindedness but a refusal to engage. Tolerance suggests leaving one another alone and that is precisely what Christians cannot do. Trevor Phillips, chairman of the Commission for Racial Equality (CRE), warned in 2005 that 'Multiculturalism suggests separateness . . . Britain is "sleep-walking" into racial segregation, with white, Muslim and black "ghettos" dividing cities.'

There is a new spirit of the age, which provides an opportunity for the Church to come into her own. The irony is that since individual preference and choice have become the cultural norm within society, parish churches have become the radical egalitarian alternative. The raison d'etre of a parish church is to bring together those who might have nothing in common other than a shared faith in Christ and a commitment to a local geographical area. It is the traditionally structured models of Church that are doing the real cross-cultural work and helping people of different race, class, gender and age to relate to one another.

Against the backcloth of the Serbian-Croatian conflict, Miroslav Volf writes:

In a post-communism, post-apartheid world people have had to learn to live with and alongside others. There are now 50 places round the globe where violence has taken root between people who share the same terrain but differ in ethnicity, race, language or religion (Volf, 1996, p. 13).

The Church stands alone in creating a climate for social change. God's mission, says Pope Francis (2013), is for a 'revolution of tenderness' through the Church. People will learn the joy of relating to Christ as the guiding light through whom all things make sense. It will be a Church that is vulnerable, bruised and hurting because it has been out on the streets and not stuck in a confine. It will be a Church that feeds the homeless, befriends those who have been divorced, and welcomes the marginalized, the disabled and the lonely.

Reflection

Collaboration in the name of social justice draws Islam and Christianity together. In my parish I have a generous exposure to different faith groups and I am richer for doing so. I meet with generosity and humour. We are a many-culture community and enjoy it for being so. A Syrian café refuses ever to charge me for my coffee because they are glad to have the Christian minister on site. An Arab restaurant provides 20 per cent discount cards for people in the church. A Muslim charity collaborates with us in our work with the homeless in the area. They provide sleeping bags for those sleeping rough, who are delighted by this gift. The Muslims provide a better quality of sleeping bag than do the Christians too!

Prayer

Lord God, thank you for sending your Son who told the Samaritan woman that she would never thirst again if she drank the water that he alone would give. Help me to drink fully from what you offer through Jesus – the way, the truth and the life – as I labour to be a living signpost to those of all faiths and none. Amen.

L

Locality

Place is integral to the identity of a church. New Testament churches are referred to by their place name. Paul writes from the Church at Colossae to give greetings to the brothers and sisters at Laodicea (Col. 4.15). The Bible talks about local churches in Galatia (1 Cor. 16.11) or in the provinces of Asia (1 Cor. 16.19). The distinctive feature of the parish church is its commitment to the locality. A core part of the Church's mission is based round the parish clergy living locally and visiting people's homes regularly.

The Church in a place is the Church for a place; the preposition 'for' is a Christological word meaning both service and transcendence. It alludes to Christ, who is both the one who came to serve and also the one through whom we see the Father (John 6.46). This offers transformation and renewal to the community of which she is is a part.

The idea of being a church for a place means more than just geographical location. The 'place' of the Church, says Newbigin (1976), is not just its situation on the surface of the globe, but its place in the fabric of human society. The word 'place' must mean the whole secular reality of the place including its physical, social, cultural and political aspects. The Church, he says, cannot be described apart from its place.

Place and story

Sheldrake (2001) and others draw a distinction between 'space' and 'place'. Space is used to refer to neutral non-empty places where the individual feels no sense of connection or belonging. Space refers to public areas such as shopping centres, airport lounges or train stations. Percy (2004) writes that place is used to refer to spaces with a story attached.

The challenge for a church leader is to create worship places rather than worship spaces, thereby bringing together people's experience of a place with the Christian narrative attached. Picturesque country churches manage this by leaving the church open and leaving a visitor's book for people to sign so that they can see how generations have been affected by, and have shaped, the church as a sacred place.

A church building provides an explicit, non-exclusive openly accessible link with the Christian narrative. Harvey (1992) wrote that the social preservation of religion as a major institution within secular societies has been in part won through the successful creation, protection and nurturing of symbolic places.

A church building upholds the notion of historicity and catholicity representing the universal to the particular and identifying the local as a part of the universal Church. The universal perspective of the Kingdom gives poignancy and perspective to the local and the particular. Pritchard (2007, p. 88) talks of church buildings as being 'the only place in a community which has a living, visible connection to the past'.

People construct their faith biographies round significant places where meaningful events have taken place. The centrality of the church building for the rites on baptism, marriage and funerals gives it a special significance for many. Inge (2003) writes that a Christian view of place will entail God, people and place having a relationship to one another in which all three are important.

The Church's task of evangelism would be a whole lot harder if there were no church buildings as a visible link to previous generations living out their Christian story. The tragedy is when the link between the church building and the Christian story is separated and the community no longer recognizes one as belonging to the other. Churches that rely on letting their church halls as a way of making contact with the wider community run the risk of being drawn into a latent consumerism and being seen simply as service providers.

In our parish we lose our immediate connection with the Christian story when we move our parent and toddler group from the church to a newly built church hall. In the church there had been a shared ownership of the group. We had pushed the altar to one side and the children were able to play during the week in the exact same spot that they would receive a blessing on Sunday. In the hall the group double in size but we lose the sense of intimacy. The idea of working with the mothers metamorphoses into a service industry whereby we are putting on activities for them. Tavinor (2007, pp. 37–40) notes that this gap between secular and sacred activities did not begin to emerge until the end of the nineteenth century. Churches began to build halls and thus social service happened outside of the liturgical area, a separation that was not found in the early or medieval Church.

Church buildings

Ours is a diverse society in need of a unifying story. This story is given a physical representation in church buildings. The missiological significance of church buildings begins fully to be realized when the buildings are connected in people's minds to the Christian narrative.

Clergy can be left feeling as if they are constantly playing catch-up with the needs of their building. The Bishop of London (Chartres, 2015) argues that church buildings are a blessing to the whole of society but a burden that falls disproportionately on the worshippers of this generation. Clergy fundraising for roof repairs are doing a job for which they are not trained in a building not fit for purpose. Rural clergy with responsibility for three or more congregations find that any sense of mission is squeezed by their responsibility for the church buildings. Volunteers who offer to mow the lawn or to clean the church are at a premium.

Church buildings in need of repair with dwindling congregations struggling to make ends meet can make church members appear to the rest of society as guardians of a heritage rather than a community of people living out the Christian story. Heritage is a frequent script connected to church buildings. Churches rely on grants from the National Heritage for successful fundraising appeals. Church of England (2010/11) statistics state that 85 per cent of people in Britain visit a church in any one year for many reasons apart from services of worship – such as weddings, funerals, school services, concerts and special events. Rylands (2005) writes that cathedrals are seen as 'the success story of the Church of England'. Attendances at regular weekly services in cathedrals have steadily increased by a total of 17 per cent since the turn of the millennium.

It is easy to feel that too much time spent in caring for the building is time wasted and that I should be caring for people rather than bricks and mortar. A drainpipe comes away from the wall and is a Health and Safety Hazard for the children in the school playground. The gutters need cleaning and a tile falls off the church roof – all this and I am only halfway through the week.

The assumption that place is immaterial is an error because it treats belief, in its corporate religious context, as more or less exclusively a mental activity. This sets up a false dichotomy between the Kingdom of God and the Church. It implies that true Christianity is a timeless truth somehow exempt from the ordinary and mundane patterns of human behaviour. It legitimizes a docetic ecclesiology whereby people can talk about being drawn to Jesus but put off by the Church.

Christianity is a mucky, earthy, dirty, elemental religion, and the running together of sacred and profane is a core part of the incarnation. I learn this myself in preparing for Sunday morning worship by picking up condoms in the churchyard and clearing away the syringes left from the Saturday night before. I fill three black dustbin liners with debris and other rubbish. The ideas from *Mission-Shaped Church* (2004) have to be put on hold. I need to start with 'Church-Shaped Church'. There are plants growing in the church guttering and the roof is in need of repair. A well-delivered sermon is not going to fix it.

The point of 'holiness' is not withdrawal from, but a way of engaging with, the realities of the world. God's holiness gave Moses the motivation for challenging the Egyptians, not the reason for withdrawing. It is transcendence understood through immanence; the glory of God expressed through the stuff of day-to-day living. It is because of this that I like going round the churchyard early on a Sunday morning with a black bin liner in hand before I celebrate the Eucharist. Liturgy and litter run hand in hand. The two somehow seem to fit together.

The Trinity is a place

There are regular theologies of time (temporal and eternal), morality, character development and relationships. A theology of place shifts the emphasis from human agency to human dependence on God, nature and the environment. Moltmann (2008) describes this as moving from eschatology to ecology – a move from the concept of time, in the progress of human history, to the concept of space, in the life-giving organism of the earth.

He writes that the Trinity is an open and inviting and uniting environment for the whole creation redeemed and renewed in God. He states that the Trinity are not only persons, but also spaces shaped by the life and indwelling of the other two. Each person of the Trinity makes itself inhabitable for the others and is moulded by their reciprocal indwelling.

The concept of Christ as an indwelling, as well as a person, means that when we are gathered together 'in Christ', he is the living space of believers (Rom. 6.3). When Paul says 'not I but Christ in me' (Gal. 2.20), by 'Christ' he means the place where believers are with all their heart and soul. When we talk of the Holy Spirit in us the Spirit is the person and we are the place of his dwelling (1 Cor. 3.6).

Reflection

I am inducted as the vicar of the parish and the bishop preaches from the parable of the great feast: the master's house will be full (Luke 14.23). This sets me dreaming of an increasing electoral roll, Sunday services full of people, and a successful church.

Some years on, the reality is different but, arguably, even better than the dream. The House has indeed become full, but not in the way I had thought it might. The lucrative pre-school and private parties have left the building, which is now an outreach and mission hub for the parish.

The church is now the local food bank, night shelter, play café, youth drop-in and church boxing outreach. We have paid for the construction of a permanent ring in our second hall. When I make an appearance and watch the punch bags rattle beneath the Sunday school memory verses pinned to the walls, I know that, despite the financial worries of the fabric, the building is host to the Christian narrative which is making unexpected inroads in the area.

Prayer

Heavenly Father, lift my eyes up from the building to the hills of the local community. Grant me wisdom and your Holy Spirit's vision to make your Son the centre of our outreach. Amen.

M

Management into mission

Management is core business for the parish priest. Without retired clergy, self-supporting ministers (SSM), clergy partners and an army of volunteers, parishes would grind to a halt. There are always bills to be paid, houses to be visited, and standing orders to be sorted. It is not possible for a church minister to exclude himself or herself from the daily grind of a parish organization. Regular and systematic financial giving is integral to a person's discipleship; a well-managed email box is a politeness towards others, not a tyranny against oneself; practical pastoral care needs an organized parish database.

The idea that a church minister can concentrate on human relationships to the exclusion of parish administration, resource management and practical jobs is docetic theology. Docetism was an early Church heresy that the humanity of Christ, his sufferings and his death were apparent rather than real. Docetism taught that if Christ were divine, he would not have actually suffered but only appeared to do so.

An early Church belief that the physical crucifixion did not actually happen becomes a modern-day belief that the day-by-day 'taking up your cross' (Luke 9.23) doesn't need to happen. It is the embodied nature of the gathered congregation that gives Christianity its shape and makes management an indispensable part of discipleship.

God's approach to management has notable successes. God turns crisis into opportunity. He raised Jesus from the dead (Acts 2.24). God makes maximum use of limited resources. Five people will chase a hundred, and a hundred will chase ten thousand (Lev. 26.8). Creation was order out of chaos and the resurrection was life out of death. God provides vision and long-term planning. He says to Abraham that his descendants will be as numerous as the stars in the sky and as the sand on the seashore (Gen. 22.17).

Jesus' approach to management during the three-year period from his baptism to his death on the cross was deep and narrow and, in human terms, not so obviously successful. He spent a lot of time with a small group of people, one of whom denied him, another of whom betrayed him, and some of whom still doubted him when it came to the ascension (Matt. 28.17).

Jesus' itinerant group of disciples was an example of what Handy (1988) calls a people-culture. A people-culture depends on trust and empathy for its effectiveness and personal conversation for communication. It is a good structure for people who know each other already. In a parish it can be divisive because it leaves some as knowledge-holders and others not knowing what is expected of them.

Richard Higginson (1996, pp. 44–51) talks of servant (Luke 22.27), steward (Luke 12.42) and shepherd (John 10.11) as three different Gospel models of management. The different roles coalesce on a Sunday morning as the minister welcomes the congregation. As a steward she has needed to make sure that people are gathering in a building where the bills have been paid, the lights are on, and the heating is working. A steward is a resource manager. She will have ensured that the Sunday school leaders are properly police checked; there is a rota for teas and coffee; and people know what is expected of them. As a servant she will know the stories of those in the congregation who are struggling. She will have visited them in the week and, as did Paul with the Philippians, she will have poured herself out like a drink offering (Phil. 2.17). As a shepherd she will teach from the pulpit and lead people in worship.

Church committees

Preparations for a church committee are as Christ-centred an activity as the conversations within. It takes time to create a context where people are willing to participate, able to contribute, and pleased to be a part of.

Committees need to avoid becoming:

- Supporters clubs (we are here simply to support the clergy).
- Abdicators (we leave it to others).
- Adversaries (we want things done our way only).

A church leader needs to:

- Offer clarity and consistency – people like to know how things stand.
- Be relationship-based as well as task-focused – people like to know what is expected of them.
- Be open to ideas and suggestions – because people like to know how they can contribute.

Committee members need to be:

- Engaged and supportive rather than disengaged supporters: represent the wider church congregation.
- Critical friends rather than unfriendly critics: share in the decision-making process and help to identify what is practical and possible.
- Active participants rather than passive observers: willing to volunteer in order to achieve what is necessary to be done.

Organizational cultures

Adirondack (1998) and Handy (1988) suggest three different organizational cultures, and a church will incorporate some of each. A leadership-focused culture is the unconscious or deliberate process whereby the environment is shaped to give the central figure as much control as possible over what goes on. The church leader has a clear idea of what needs to be done and invests a huge amount of time in seeing it come to fruition. Commonly used words for this culture are 'vision' or 'calling', with a central figure as the decision-maker. A leadership culture may emerge where the running of the church is clergy-dependent through lack of other volunteers.

A clergy-dependent leadership culture will plateau because there are only so many people with whom the person can form a relationship and only so long that he can continue in an unsupported role. The role will remain pertinent with the need for a central figure to ensure continuity, provide direction and to look after vulnerable members of the congregation.

In a people-focused culture congregation members take initiatives and feel responsible for their area of work. This culture emphasizes mutual aid, friendship and involvement of members in one another's lives. When there is too much emphasis on a people-focused culture the management of the church becomes overly dependent on certain individuals. The key to success is having like-minded people who recognize, support and work for a set of common aims. The organizational culture can appear confusing to someone unused to the way things work. A church with significant lay leadership operates a people-focused culture. It marks an end to the days of parishes as individual fiefdoms where everything is dependent on or decided by the vicar.

A role-culture is where the tasks are identified and people are sought to fulfil those roles. There will always be a need for a treasurer, an Alpha co-ordinator or a children's worker. The role is usually so described that a range of individuals could fill it. A role-culture ensures that activities are a part of a wider corporate whole – lessons are learnt and objectives are secured. If there is too much emphasis on a role-culture some people will become frustrated at the discussion that needs to go into making a decision.

The advantages of this type of culture are that it is inclusive of people and diversity friendly. People are able to volunteer because they know what they are putting themselves forward for. A church where volunteers are involved in leadership, and where roles are rotated regularly, is likely to be growing – especially where younger members and new members are included in lay leadership and service.

The ultimate purpose of mission management is evangelism, enabling people to come face to face with the living God. Percey (2014) writes that there is a temptation to put mission and maintenance in opposition. Maintenance is equated with simply keeping the show on the road, a sort of status quo, which lacks vision. When this happens, maintenance is cast as a drag on the real work of the church, a hindrance to the proper work of mission.

Trinitarian management

There is a trinitarian formula to mission management. In a parish there will be a vision for what needs to be done. There will be volunteers willing to do it. There is a church fellowship, out of whom the volunteers are drawn, and from among whom the vision will have been nurtured. The vision comes from the Father's love – what plans do we need to make to put God's love into practice in the context in which we find ourselves (1 John 4.7–8)? The volunteers are the Son of God's love embodying the vision – how do we follow Jesus' example in putting this vision into practice (John 13.14)? The church fellowship is God the Holy Spirit's love – how do we keep the unity of the Spirit through the bond of peace (Eph. 4.1–6)? Vision, volunteers and fellowship are the Father, Son and Holy Spirit formula that shapes the Church.

Trinitarian ecclesiology is Christ-centred and outward-looking. Mission and management are held together in discipleship. The former provides the vision and the latter the substance for the work of the Church. Making disciples is time heavy and labour intensive. Making relationships with people is hard work; its benefits are often long term and not immediately apparent. Management into mission is not a slipstreamed organizational efficiency, but a long-term relationship-building exercise.

Mission

Creating a division between mission and ecclesiology does not do justice to the essential missionary nature of a Christ-centred and outward-looking church. The parish church is naturally heterogeneous in drawing people together from across the local community. Old people's groups, youth clubs and Sunday school are expected subdivisions of an inherited church structure.

The question for a parish church is how she might love, cherish and nurture the liturgical, sacramental and congregational treasures she has been given while also creating different points of access and different cultural experiences of church for others. Jesus may have created a new humanity out of Jew and Gentile yet both still continued to speak separate languages and to live in different socio-economic circumstances (Eph. 2.15). Oneness in Christ contains within it an ongoing diversity that is worked through in the pews of the parish church.

Parish churches offer opportunities to gather together diverse groups from across the community. It is the counter-cultural nature of a parish church that guarantees its relevance to society. We live in a society of perfect means and muddled ends. The parish church is the reverse – the church calls people into a living relationship with Christ but the process is overlaid with trad-itional structures of a church culture that does not easily chime with contemporary society. It is the collective nature of the parish church that is its distinguishing feature.

Believing Christians, happy agnostics, interested atheists, noisy children, the poor, the vulnerable and the disaffected all have a place of their own and are able to find their own levels of belong-ing. In Augustine's (1.35) *City of God* the visible Church on earth is a mixed community, saints and sinners side by side. The citizens of the two cities will be separated at the last judgement, but for now they mingle together.

Paul thanks the Philippian church for the partnership in the gospel (Phil. 1.5). Partnership with all different types of church is a key skill for the parish clergy. Grace Davie (Davie, 2008, pp. 154–5) talks of there being two religious economies, which run side by side in modern Europe. The first is the historical geographically based parochial system. The second is voluntary and associational, which comes as a shift from a culture of obligation to a culture of choice. A partnership between associational and geographical churches requires parish churches to live happily with other expressions of Christian community. Vincent Donovan's work with the Masai tribe has been significant in how mission literature has developed. He wrote that: 'The missionary's job is to preach, not the church, but Christ. If he preaches Christ and the message of Christianity, the church may well appear, but it might not be the church he had in mind' (Donovan, 1982, p. 81).

In my parish we have one 'missional community' meeting in a pub and another in a person's home. There is also a new church plant located in our church hall. Our Sunday morning parish Eucharist is one among a panoply of options for people in the area. The parish church is the matrix supporting, nurturing or simply being friend to other types of church gatherings in the area.

Reflection

The day everyone starts to enjoy PCC is when it moves from being a gathering of occasional church business colleagues to being a body able to develop into a Jesus-centred fellowship. This came about in my parish through a change in venue for people to meet. When a single mother joins the PCC, meetings move from the church function room to her beautiful home. Each member sits around the family table in a warm, lived-in space. Years of leadership-focused institutional formality give way to a people-focused – albeit still clergy-led – culture. People tell their stories of how they came to attend the church. Some open up about life's joys and struggles. My management has become an exercise in nurturing other people's relationships.

Prayer

Thank you, living Lord, that you bring order out of chaos. Thank you that you set eternity in our hearts. Thank you for the range of skills you give us both to manage the practicalities of your Church and to be the Bride for your Son. Amen.

N

Narrative theology

There is a Nicodemus in all of us looking for new ways of understanding God (John 3). The sheer recklessness of the cross demands
a response. A narrative approach to Scripture wants the Bible to
be understood through its stories rather than simply through
definitive statements of right and wrong or notional propositions
of truth. The gospel is not about abstract ideas of love, but about
the story of Jesus Christ. We are not formed by rules, but by
narratives. Stories give our lives coherence and character. In his
Summa Theologica, Thomas Aquinas tells us that theology is
not a science because it deals with individual persons and events
such as Abraham, Isaac and Jacob. A science does not deal with
individual cases but with general and universal principles.

A narrative approach to theology is not a science, but nor is
it a pathway to subjectivism. It provides the context for credal
beliefs, which in turn provide the framework for narrative truth.
The Creeds are a distillation of systematic theology and provide
an authoritative stance on the Christian faith. They are the posts
that mark out the boundaries of a field. A narrative approach to
theology inhabits the hermeneutical spaces within the field. It is
within that space communities of faith interpret and live out the
stories from the Bible.

Scripture conveys truth through such literary forms as poetry,
parable, historical narrative, visionary apocalyptic, praise, mock-
ing, satire, irony, prophecy, wisdom sayings and so on. Over
70 per cent of the Bible consists of stories. Adding poetry and
proverbs leaves probably less than 10 per cent abstract 'intellectual' content. Stories help people to interpret and make sense
of what happens to them and work out their responses.

John's Gospel was the last of the four Gospels to be written. It
is more propositional and conclusion-driven than the more narra-

tive-based Synoptics. The contrast is shown in the reasons for the Gospels being written. John was written so that the reader might believe that Jesus is the Messiah, the Son of God (John 20.31). Luke was written simply to provide an orderly account of all that had happened (Luke 1.2).

With a narrative approach to the Bible we can read ourselves into the script as if it were an unfolding story. This can result in multiple yet not contradictory readings. A narrative approach suggests that Isaiah 7.14 would not originally have been connected to the person of Christ born to a virgin hundreds of years later; yet the virgin birth of Jesus also fulfils Isaiah 7.14. We understand how an eighth-century BC audience understood what had happened, and then we recognize the freedom of later readers to interpret those texts differently in the light of later events.

In Scripture the Israelites learn the character of God by remembering the stories of what he has done. They are told to remember that they were slaves in Egypt and that the LORD God redeemed them (Deut. 15.15). The Bible talks of God as he interacts with Abraham (Gen. 26.4), Moses (Ex. 3.14), David (2 Sam. 7.8–10) and Jesus (Matt. 3.17). In the early Church Barnabas and Paul told the Council of Jerusalem the stories of what had happened to them in order to persuade the members not to insist on the circumcision of Gentile converts (Acts 15).

Narrative theology, popularized by Stanley Hauerwas (1981), sees the stories of God found in Scripture as being re-enacted in the life of the local church. God's engagement with the Israelites and the early Church are prototype encounters for his engagement with society today. Theology is an unfolding story rather than simply a series of propositional truths. The fundamental category of human flourishing is not freedom but knowing the narrative of which one is a part: 'The Scriptures tell the story of the forgiving love of God and the church is an extended argument over time about the significance of that story and how to interpret it' (Hauerwas, 1981, p. 39).

Looking at the Bible through the lens of narrative as opposed to systematizing the Scripture is accepting contrasting interpretative voices. Biblical stories are multi-vocal. It is possible to have contrasting readings of the same story held alongside one another within the same Christian community.

The parable of the talents is an example of how this is so. A man lent his three slaves money before going away on a journey. Two of them made a profit from his investment; the third made no attempt to do so and was deemed wrong for not having tried (Matt. 25.14–30). The most familiar interpretation of the parable is that we should use whatever 'talent' God has given us.

Herzog (1994, pp. 150–68) offers an alternative explanation: the third servant is the 'good guy' refusing to play along with someone whose only interest is in making money. The master is described as a 'harsh' man: someone who was willing to 'harvest where he had not sown'. In the minds of those listening to Jesus this could have suggested an absentee landlord: someone willing to charge high rent and to confiscate people's lands (and hence their harvests) when they could not pay. The third servant refused to collude with his master's greed; he exposed the sham of how the other servants had behaved in allowing themselves to be used for his exploitative purposes.

Under Herzog's interpretation, the point of the parable is the political subversion of the third slave rather than the return on their investment for the first two. Both readings of the story are valid because they enable different communities of believers to encounter the risen Lord in the pages of Scripture.

When Peter denied Jesus three times, was he more angry than frightened? A conventional reading would say the latter. However, Peter had been brave enough to draw his sword in front of the Roman guards in Gethsemane. He had had the courage to follow Jesus and to sit in the courtyard waiting for events to take their course. His response to being questioned might have come from exasperation at the situation in which they found themselves. The point is that each story supports different interpretations.

Our task is to live out our twenty-first-century version of the stories in the Bible. Hauerwas and Gregory Jones (1990) write that Christian narrative theology provided by the community of faith is the most appropriate context in which to 'do' theology. It is a clarion call to the parishes. We are our stories (Crossley, 2000). Evangelism comes when we lend people our story so that they can decide whether they want to keep it as their own. We encounter the risen Christ through the pages of Scripture, as a part of a Christian community in the process of engagement with society.

Our mission as the Church is to carry God's redemption story on into our own cultural contexts faithfully and consistently with the account given in the Bible. The Bible's story illustrates a relationship between God and his people and we live this out in concert with each other: 'The point is to look at God, look at yourself and to ask where you are in the story . . . when we say thank you to God we connect our own experience with God as giver' (Williams, 2014, p. 28).

Biblical narrative comes before both evangelical proposition and liberal interpretation, in the same way that listening comes before talking. Narrative theology creates a context for dialogue rather than debate. Debate is oppositional: two sides oppose each other and attempt to prove each other wrong. Dialogue is collaborative: two or more sides work together towards a common understanding. Bretherton (2010) writes that Christians should treat conflict as an occasion for hospitality, as an opportunity to display 'interpretative charity' – the challenge is ours!

God's weakness draws each generation of the Church into his ongoing story of redemption (1 Cor. 2.1–5). God asks us to be like him (Eph. 5.1–2), and invites us to talk with him (Matt. 7.7). He promises us redemption (Rom. 3.23–24), and our new redeemed self is created according to the likeness of God (Eph. 4.24). God is literally present in and through the lives of the people who gather in his name. We become a part of him and he becomes a part of us.

Biblical narrative is the truth of God in action and underpins our moments of decision-making, life predicaments or new journeys of faith. We all have a Nicodemus within us looking for new ways to understand God. We are 'Thomas' wanting to be convinced. We are 'Simon Peter' wanting reassurance. We are 'Judas' wanting to control. The stories shape us as we grow into the people that God wants us to become. Oakley (2016) writes that God's gift to us is our being. The gift we are asked to give in return is our becoming who we become in our life. We indwell the baptism story. Baptism is an attitude as well as an event. Jesus describes his coming passion as a baptism that he has to undergo (Luke 12.50). You expect to find baptized Christians on the edge of chaos where need is at its most intense.

We become Christ's body. Sunday by Sunday the congregation learns to be humble, gentle and patient with one another (Eph.

4.2), and the Church brings together people who would otherwise have been separated through social and economic circumstances. Maisy and Amber were six-year-olds who had been best friends, but lost contact when Amber had gone to a different school. They meet up again when both of their parents come to my church. They are both so pleased to see each other that they sit in silence throughout the service, each looking at the other and saying nothing.

A parish church is built on the fragility of recently made relationships, the loyalty of the long-standing members and the possibilities represented in gathering people together in the name of Christ. A believing, celebrating and loving Christian congregation, rooted in Christ, committed to each other and invested in the life of the community will not be able to withhold from others the secret of its hope.

Reflection

Two single parents, both with sad stories of love lost, make sandwiches in the night shelter which offers space to people with no homes of their own. They are volunteers who understand what it is to be vulnerable, both through their own experiences and through their love of the vulnerable Christ who did not resist the torture of the cross. They put their backs into the work, laughing and chatting, setting the tables and chopping vegetables. They are glad because they know that despite their own hardships, their efforts are making a difference to the lives of needy people. The narrative of the bruised Messiah lives on through what they do, getting their hands dirty, giving encouragement to others, and being faithful to the call of Christ on their lives.

Prayer

Heavenly Father, you lead and I will follow. Help me to take part in your mission of tenderness and love through the Church today and in the coming week. Amen.

O

Older people and families

Why do churches worry about the young people who don't go to church, but not celebrate the old who do? There are step-by-step plans for how to get more young people into churches but the presence of older people in the congregation is taken for granted. We are constantly told that the age profile of church members is increasing, and so the oldies are treated like a consolation prize – 'there might not be many young people in church', we think, 'but at least old people still come'. Congregations are themselves made the scapegoat for the lack of new members; they are criticized for being too old, too few or too set in their ways.

There is a silver-haired revolution in such churches and they would do well to take note. If congregations want money raised, committees manned or projects run, it will be done by those in their sixties – 60 is the new 40. It is this demographic that often makes a significant contribution to the community. Those in their sixties are reliable financial givers and volunteer with midweek church projects. They are more than just cake-bakers – the silver generation has become the new youth workers.

Theology of old age

There is a need for a theology of old age to help to counter a soft ageism within the Church: 'Teach the older men to be temperate, worthy of respect, self-controlled, and sound in faith, in love and in endurance' (Titus 2.2).

Personhood is the irrevocable gift and call of God, no matter someone's age. There is now not only a third age, but a fourth age. There are the 'young old' (65–74), the 'old' (75–85) and the 'very old' (85+). Elders today are pioneers – exploring for us all what it might mean to live in an ageing society. 'Old men ought to be explorers', said T. S. Eliot, '. . . love is most nearly itself when here and now cease to matter'.

Ageing cannot be understood simply in terms of what it is not: not young or energetic; not productively employed; not having much more of life ahead. A loss of self-awareness due to Alzheimer's does not equate to a loss of self. We are more than just our physical or mental abilities. What is crucial to maintaining personhood is the quality of the person's relationships. In the words of the Carly Simon song, 'nobody does it better' than the Church. The gift that older people bring to society is the chance for us to build relationships with our future self. Ageing well is part of living well. A society uncomfortable with old age is a society uneasy with death. A society uneasy with death is yet to be touched by the healing hand of Christ.

God is both young and old. With the Lord, 'a day is like a thousand years, and a thousand years are like a day' (2 Peter 3.8). The kingdom of heaven belongs to the children who ran up to Jesus, but also to Anna, the 84-year-old widow who never left the temple but worshipped night and day, praying and fasting (Luke 2.37).

Families

Soon after my ordination I went back to my childhood church to preach. I wanted the people who had known me all of my life to understand what I was doing. Jesus did likewise. He went home to Nazareth and preached in the synagogue because he wanted to start his mission in the place where he had grown up. What did it mean to him that his family thought him mad and that he was also a prophet without honour in his own country (Mark 3.21, 6.4)? Mark's Gospel says: 'He could not do any miracles there, except lay his hands on a few people who were ill and heal them. He was amazed at their lack of faith' (Mark 6.5–6).

Families remain a point of reference throughout our lives. Whatever plaudits I might receive for my preaching, I will always value more a favourable word from my mother. The universality of the mother's role is shown by the fact that all world languages have the consonant 'm' – making the sound of the baby's cry – in their word for 'mother'.

Collins-Mayo, Mayo and Nash (2010) identify that the family is as important, and in some instances more so, as friends to Generation Y. This remains so even when parents divorce. Intimacy replaces security and children look on their parents in friendship terms.

The closeness between young people and their families is reflected in patterns of church attendance. Voas and Crockett (2005) tell us that if neither parent attends church at least once a month, the chances of the child doing so are negligible: less than 3 per cent. If both parents attend at least monthly, there is a 46 per cent chance that the child will do so. Where just one parent attends, the likelihood is halved to 23 per cent.

Churches run parent and toddler groups to interact with families in the community. A provision for children and young people draws in parents in their twenties and thirties who will then provide the backbone of the future church membership.

Families in the Bible

Jesus' Israel was a collectivist culture that adhered to an extended, rather than a nuclear, family model. Multi-generational families with at least three generations living together were common. In our contemporary culture privacy is more highly valued and economic prosperity has created opportunities for greater privacy.

The words for 'nuclear family' do not appear in Scripture; the term 'household' is used instead. A 'household' (*oikos*) was the basic unit of society in the New Testament. It included the extended family (wife, children, friends, relatives and slaves). Cornelius and his household were gathered, 'to listen to everything the Lord has commanded you [Peter] to tell us' (Acts 10.33). Upon hearing the gospel preached by Peter, everyone in Cornelius' household believed and was baptized (Acts 11.15–18).

The parenting role was shared among responsible adults and was not the sole property of the mother and father. On her way back from Jerusalem when Mary could not find Jesus, it did not occur to her that he would not be with other friends or relatives

(Luke 2.41–52). In biblical times girls were married at the age of puberty. This is an age that in our contemporary Western society would be considered child abuse. The difference between then and now is that the wife would never have been on her own as she might be today in a nuclear family unit. She would always have been among other adults, and the husband would never have been in a position to take unfair advantage of her situation.

The Bible is unequivocal about the importance of marriage but, other than the centrality of a monogamous and faithful relationship and the bringing up of children, is largely unpre-scriptive about what socially constructed form this family will take. Marriage is to last a lifetime: people getting married are to be faithful to one another 'as long as [they] both shall live'. It is within the safe confines of the marital bond between husband and wife that children can be conceived, born and nurtured. God said to the man and woman, 'Be fruitful and multiply' (Gen. 1.28). The mutual devotion between husband and wife is a reflection of God's devotion to his people: 'For this reason a man will leave his father and mother and be united to his wife, and the two will become one flesh.' This is a profound mystery – but I am talking about Christ and the church (Eph. 5.31–32).

Contemporary families

The fierce debate over same-sex marriages has clouded more significant family issues for the Church to consider. The real con-cern for the Church is not the difference between civil partnership and marriage, but the fact that Britain has the highest divorce rate in the EU – almost twice the EU average – and that many children from broken homes are unhappy.

The effects of adultery are devastating. A couple that I married 20 years previously find me via Google, and come to visit me. I have not seen them since their wedding day. They want to return to the person (me) with whom the marriage had begun to see if the damage done by the husband's affair can be repaired. The fact of them reaching out to me, after that significant period of time, shows the responsibility that the Church has in people's marriages as a result of a parish priest conducting their wedding.

In 2007 UNICEF ranked child wellbeing in Britain as the lowest of 21 industrialized countries. The Children's Society, in 2012, found that at any given moment, 1 in 11 children in the UK aged between 8 and 15 have a low sense of wellbeing. And according to the Office for National Statistics (ONS), 1 in 10 children in the UK aged between 5 and 16 has a clinically diagnosed mental health disorder.

A nuclear family is in origin an economic unit emerging out of the Industrial Revolution. Women dealt with the domestic sphere, and men the public sphere. Given that the nuclear family was originally an economic unit, as soon as both partners begin to work the economic rationale for the union begins to break down. Some families will move back towards an extended family unit, drawing on grandparents or buying back, in the shape of a nanny or an au pair, the extra people needed to support the parents' dual incomes; some children left both in a breakfast club and an after-school club can have as long a 'working day' as their parents.

The parish church is a household

The multi-generational household model of extended family is replicated in a parish church. A parish church offers a household as a model of family living. This supports parents by widening their understanding of the nuclear family, and modelling an extended family. Nuclear families become de facto 'households' through being immersed in a local church, and are strengthened through being so. In multi-generational church communities, young people are offered encouragement and learn from the stories of others. Parents are given support and older people companionship – each age group benefits the other.

Marriages are put under pressure by the unquestioned assumptions of the nuclear family unit and the uncomfortable way that it fits with much of modern-day living. An opportunity to cultivate an extended family structure to supplement and strengthen the core nuclear family unit can develop naturally into an invitation to come to church and to meet with members of the congregation. A missionary call on the Church to offer parenting support and companionship is one that a parish church is well placed to meet.

Thatcher (2007, p. 202) talks of churches worldwide having much to do in recognizing stepfamilies as a growing family form. He talks of the need for the Church to support 'blended families'; these might include a whole new configuration of relationships – an able-bodied person caring for a declining friend or partner; single-parent families with the parent trying to be both mother and father to their children. The issue for the single parent is poverty, not nurture. Single-parent families can draw others into the parenting process and do so by becoming a member of a church congregation. Beck-Gernsheim (2002, p. 34) refers to these non-traditional forms of family living as 'patchwork' families. Children, families and youth work are integral parts of a church's service of her community.

Making links across generations and supporting the role of the parents is a core task for a local parish church. Child Protection issues notwithstanding, a primary resource that the church can offer to young people is the opportunity for them to build nurturing and supportive relationships with adults. Parent and toddler groups are a frequent way in which churches engage with their communities. The parish church becomes the UK equivalent of the African proverb that states that it takes a village to raise a child. Family life is a vital concern for society and a missionary imperative for the Church.

Reflection

I am leader and servant of the local Christian household. People ask me for advice. They want my teaching, prayers and good counsel. I am expected not only to provide a vision for the household, but also to pick up all the tasks still to be done when volunteer power runs out. Putting out the chairs for the Sunday morning service, as well as giving the sermon for the future of the household, is that to which I am called. I fulfil my ordinal vows as both CEO and cleaner in the house of God through doing so.

Prayer

Heavenly Father, help me to lead and to follow, to advise and to trust, to play my part in your household with authority and humility. Amen.

P

Prayer

Prayer is the bread and butter work of the clergy. A parish may not demand its clergy to be good at admin, but will always expect them to pray. Origen prayed three times a day. The Psalmists prayed seven times daily (Ps. 119.164). The salient point is that we are to pray regularly (1 Thess. 5.17).

In the Old Testament people pray

- on their knees (1 Kings 8.54);
- bowing (Ex. 4.1);
- on their faces before God (2 Chron. 20.18; Matt. 26.39);
- standing (1 Kings 8.22).

In the New Testament Jesus prayed both in public (John 11.41–42) and alone (Matt. 14.23). He got up to pray while it was still dark (Mark 1.35). He prayed in lonely places (Luke 5.16). He prayed all night (Luke 6.12). He prayed before meals (Matt. 26.26), before important decisions (Luke 6.12), and before and after healing people (Mark 7.34; Luke 5.16). If Jesus wanted to pray that much then how much more so I need to. When I pray at the start of the day, I am stripping myself down to the bare canvas for what people want of me. Praying and living out the Lord's Prayer is the height of my ambition for a day in the parish.

John Wesley travelled 250,000 miles on horseback, averaging 20 miles a day, for 40 years. He preached 40,000 sermons, produced 400 books, and knew 10 languages. At 83 he was annoyed that he couldn't write for more than 15 hours a day without straining his eyes, and at 86 he was ashamed that he could not preach more than twice a day! He complained in his diary that there was an increasing tendency to lie in bed till 5.30 a.m. I have so much to do that I must spend several hours in prayer before I can do it.

What is prayer?

Intercessory prayer is the distinctive prayer of the clergy – praying in the parish, for the community, and with people. Intercessory prayer is our waiting on God on behalf of others. Waiting is a regular feature of parish life, which is relationship-based rather than task-driven. Pausing for others is a natural part of the week-by-week rhythm of a church.

Waiting for God is a central theme of Scripture. The prophets wait thousands of years for the Messiah (Isa. 7.14); Simeon waited his whole life before encountering the baby Jesus in the temple (Luke 2.22–40). The virgins waited until midnight for the bridegroom to appear (Matt. 25). The disciples waited in the city for the Holy Spirit to come (Luke 24.49). 'We wait in hope for the LORD; he is our help and our shield' (Ps. 33.20).

The church building represents the waiting of the generations. Waiting for anything is a counter-cultural activity. It does not fit naturally into a society where people want things done imme-diately and on their own terms. In the minibus after a weekend residential, a young person announces, 'I want chips and I want them now!'

We wait for people we love. The anticipatory waiting of the mothers at a school gate is one such example. The climax of Dostoevsky's book *Crime and Punishment* is another. Sonia is waiting for Raskolnikov to be released from prison. She waits near the prison fence to talk with him and bring him gifts during his daily hour of exercise. It is when Sonia is ill and unable to visit that he finds himself missing her and waiting with anxious concern. It is while waiting for her that he recognizes that he loves her. At the end of the book there is a moment of enlightenment where Raskolnikov realizes that Sonia truly loves him and will wait for him while he is in prison:

> Both of them looked pale and thin; but in these ill, pale faces there now gleamed the dawn of a renewed future, a complete recovery to a new life. What had revived them is love, the heart of one containing an infinite source of life for the heart of the other ... They determined to wait and endure (Dostoevsky, 1991, p. 629).

There is more to prayer than simply listing the tasks for the day and asking for God's blessing on what we were going to do anyway. Our cravings as a human being don't become prayer just because it is God we ask to attend to them. If we are list-praying we will learn nothing more of God than our own perceptions of what is important.

There is more to prayer than the words themselves. Christianity is never at a loss for words. There are the treasures of the Scriptures, the liturgy and the wisdom of the ages for us to enjoy. Morning and evening prayer provide liturgical steerage through the changes of the day. The tradition of our faith shows us how the glorious words of God echo down the generations. People coming towards the end of their lives have the poetry of the ages and the thoughts of the saints to comfort them and to guide them through their last days.

Away from words, I am most fluent with silence and solitude. It is in silence that we pray most ardently, for in the silence of the heart God speaks. If we want to pray we must learn to listen. I like to sit on my own in the church for half an hour at the start of the day in order to push back the busyness that clamours for my attention, and to create space for the Holy Spirit to take root. T. S. Eliot talks of how words strain, crack, and sometimes break, under the burden. He talks of how silence comes as an underground train stops too long between stations and the conversation rises and slowly fades into silence. It is in the silences that punctuate the day that I find myself most able to pray.

I have a sabbatical and take it as an opportunity to spend a month alone in a cottage on the coast. Parish life is relationship-heavy and I feel God calling me into a period of solitude. Just as Jesus emptied himself, out of love for us (Phil. 2.17), I want to empty myself out of my love for God. I am like a child learning to pray for the first time. I sit for a whole day on the beach watching the tide go out, and then I wait for it to come back in.

I sit, with no mobile phone to distract me, for a whole morning under a tree watching the progress of the day. Prayer offers a different relationship with time. Praying time is not a commodity to be maximized, but a gift that is given. God is endlessly generous. He gives us days to play with and when those are finished he gives us another.

Lewin (2009) expresses the different relationship with time that I experienced during the long days on my own before my return to parish life:

Prayer is like watching for the
Kingfisher
All you can do is
Be where he is likely to appear, and
Wait.
Often, nothing much happens;
There is space, silence and
Expectancy.
No visible sign, only the
Knowledge that he's been there
And may come again.
Seeing or not seeing cease to matter,
You have been prepared.
But sometimes, when you've almost
Stopped expecting it, a flash of brightness
Gives encouragement.

We pray to be like Christ because he prayed to be like us

There are two ways in which we approach a holy and transcendent God (Isa. 6). We come before God in either worship or repentance. We either rejoice in God's grace (Matt. 5.12) or we grieve because of sin (Matt. 5.4). Each is a distancing of ourselves from God. It is a recognition that God is gloriously and wholly different to who we are. Each is a recognition that our moral worth does not come from our religious practice, but through the space that we make for the work of the Holy Spirit.

God will not work round the Church but instead works through it. The more aligned we are to his will, the more readily the Holy Spirit permeates the relationships of which we are a part. We pray to change our feelings rather than God's mind. Paul prayed for a fuller knowledge of God, but never for a change in people's circumstances (Eph. 1.15–19). Events run their course, but reach a conclusion quicker if they are aligned with God's will.

Abraham pleads for Sodom and Gomorrah, not because he is trying to change God's mind but because he is opening up a new reality of which he and the righteous in the city are a part (Gen. 18.22–33). In the parish we pray for those who are sick not because we want a quick fix, but because we want our prayers to be a part of God's unfolding order. Is it so hard to believe that the human will is built into creation as a force in the structure of being, so that believing prayer and prayerful obedience actually does (to use the cliché) 'change things'?

Prayer is the point at which our spiritual yearning matches up with Christ's vulnerability. We pray to be like Christ, and in his incarnation he prayed to be like us. Gregory of Nicea wrote that it's not only that we are called to be imitators of God, but also that God is being asked to be an imitator of us. We pray to be like Christ because he prayed to be like us, and so connected with our human condition. Jesus learned obedience from what he suffered (Heb. 5.8). We learn faith through what we endure (James 1.3).

Keep on praying

Television is no reason not to pray. People often spend longer in a day watching television than they will in a week on prayer. A 2010 ICM Poll identified that the average television viewing for an adult in the UK in 2010 was more than 30 hours a week, or over four hours a day. No one is going to learn about the grace of God from the *News at Ten*.

Boredom is no reason to stop praying. Boredom is creative and prayer is subversive because each imagines how things could be different to how they are now. I owe much of my creativity to long, melancholic and boring holidays as a child. Gentle boredom can be a pathway to rich times of prayer. It is simple to work through a set liturgy, a list of those for whom we want to pray and to exhaust any ideas we may have for what is important. It is then easy to feel that our prayers are done, to say 'Amen', and to conclude.

A period of low-level boredom is an invitation to pray for longer and works our way through to the tenderness and peace of God. T. S. Eliot writes that prayer is more than an order of words, the conscious occupation of the praying mind, or the sound of the voice praying. These are only hints and guesses, hints followed by guesses; and the rest is prayer, observance, discipline, thought and action.

Distractions are no reason to stop praying. How will we ever learn to push away the busy thoughts, selfish yearnings and limiting images that perennially crowd our minds? As the Book of Common Prayer puts it, we have followed too much the devices and desires of our own hearts . . . and there is no health in us. Distractions can become a pathway to discipline. Prayer is a lengthy and often tough process by which our scrambled selves are brought in tune with God's perfect self. Jesus is at the right hand of God interceding for us, and so we are in good company (Rom. 8.34).

When our prayer life is squeezed our spirituality grows arid. Busy days become pale reflections of one another. The danger of admiring people who work hard is that busyness and virtue become equated with each other. In the parish there are always jobs to be done – bills to be paid, emails to be answered, and people to be visited. Without the anchor of time spent in prayer, we end up feeling that however much we do, it is not enough. Running a parish is the equivalent of managing a small business. The challenge is to be Martha in action but Mary in attitude (Luke 10.38–42).

Reflection

When opportunity arises I go into the church on my own. Standing on the same spot from which I preach on Sundays, I read the Bible slowly and pray. The place from which I give vision and encouragement to others becomes the place in which I sense the Holy Spirit giving vision and encouragement to me. I ask the Father to help me to keep Jesus at the centre of my plans for the church. I pray for those who are involved, for the endurance required, and for clear communication to the people in the parish. I then walk down the aisle and go home, but I cannot stop praying – even when the ideas stop flowing. The Father and I are both enjoying the intimacy.

Prayer

Heavenly Father, thank you that my prayers are pieces of your puzzle and that I am able to find myself where I belong, in Jesus' name, Amen.

Q

Quota

In the Church of England ministry and identity are shaped by a relational link beyond the immediately local. Key responsibilities for teaching and tradition, as well as maintenance and buildings, come from our shared commitment to one another through the diocese. Quota, parish share and common fund are different names to describe the same thing. Each congregation member pledges money to the parish. Each parish contributes towards diocesan expenditure. Each diocese supports the budget for the Archbishops' Council. The volunteer hours put in by parish treasurers could power a rocket to the moon.

Money in the Bible

The Bible offers 500 verses on prayer and 2,000 verses on money. Jesus' parables are rich with financial imagery. There is the pearl of great price (Matt. 13.45–46) and the lost coin (Luke 15.8–10). The prodigal son squanders his inheritance (Luke 15.11–32); the rich man, in the story of Lazarus, misuses his wealth (Luke 16.19–31).

Jesus' teaching looks at the dark side of money, acknowledging its capacity to turn people inwards on themselves rather than outwards towards others. It is easier for a camel to pass through the eye of a needle than for a rich man to enter the Kingdom of God (Luke 18.25); to whom much is given, much is expected (Luke 12.48). In addition, Paul writes that the love of money is the root of evil (1 Tim. 6.10).

Jesus' ministry benefited from the financial giving of others. Women whom he had healed followed him and were helping to support him and his disciples' ministry out of their own means

(Luke 8.1–3). After Jesus' death Joseph of Arimathea and Nico-demus both expressed their commitment in financial terms. The former placed Jesus in his own tomb (Matt. 27.60) and the latter bought 35 kilos of myrrh and aloes (John 19.39).

For us, the use of money is an exercise in discipleship. Trad-ition has it that Martin Luther said, 'There are three conversions a person needs to experience: The conversion of the head, the conversion of the heart, and the conversion of the pocketbook.' Our diaries and our bank statements are sacraments of our dis-cipleship. They give a material shape to what we say about our commitment to follow Jesus. Discipleship is a shared enterprise exercised as a part of a Christian community. Money might be the first word, but it is never the last. Just as work is in the context of the Sabbath, so is money in the context of relationships with others.

Jesus' use of miracles offers an illustration for how this is so. In the Gospels Jesus' miracles always happen in response to faith from others. The man with leprosy threw himself at Jesus' feet and begged to be healed (Luke 5.12). The centurion asked Jesus to heal his daughter because he recognized Jesus' authority (Matt. 8.8–9). Jesus' miracles were not simply a dramatic performance, as would have been him throwing himself off the highest point of the temple have been (Luke 4.9). His miracles, as does the Church's use of her money, happen in the context of relationships with others.

A common purse

A common purse pays for the administration of the church com-munity, underwriting its expenses, supporting its mission, and alleviating hardship. Ageing clergy are a long time retired, and pensions need to be paid. Church buildings need to be maintained. Poorer parishes, of which mine is one, need to be supported. I find myself in a conundrum of bricks and mortar: the boiler floods every time there is rain. Tree roots block long-neglected Victorian drains. This means that any rainfall is unable to drain away and instead it is forced back up the pipes into the boiler room, leaving a lethal combination of water, electricity and gas. For good measure the school has stored old desks and tables in the boiler room and so there is wood to fuel whatever explosion may happen. Something needs to be done quickly. At best the boiler will simply flood and the church will be left icy. The previous winter, people stood shivering in warm winter coats, their breath frosty against the cold. At worst the boiler will explode; it is a health and safety nightmare. I ring the diocese and tell them that someone could die if something is not done. They promise to come and have a look at it.

A common purse enables a church to exercise a commitment to the community and a concern for the welfare of others. The open heart of the church and the social needs of the area meet on a regular basis with the homeless people who knock on my door. Brian has been released from prison with nowhere to stay the night. He and I sit past midnight eating chicken and chips together, waiting for a caseworker to arrive to take him to a night shelter. The food, drink and clothes, that we will be asked on the last day by the Son of Man whether we provided, all cost money to secure – 'whatever you did for one of the least of these brothers and sisters of mine, you did for me' (Matt. 25.40).

A common purse is a collective voice able to promote justice within society. In the agrarian economy of Old Testament times there was not the same distance between money and worker as there is in a market economy. Capital was not the money paid into your account at the end of the month, but the food that you ate with your family. The intention for the society was to prevent the concentration of wealth and make sure that each family had the means to feed itself. One-tenth of the harvest should be shared with immigrants, orphans and widows (Deut. 14.28–29). Money should be lent at no interest to those in need (Ex. 22—25). Debts should be cancelled every seventh year (Deut. 15.1–2, 7–11). Every fiftieth year was to be a year of jubilee during which property was to be returned to the family of the original owner. In the New Testament tithing is referred to, but not commanded as such. Giving is to be done cheerfully, generously and according to one's circumstances (2 Cor. 9.6–7; James 1.17; Luke 21.1–4).

The Church tackles social injustice by creating social capital (Putnam, 2000). Social capital is a specialism of the parish church whose raison d'être is to gather people together – 'I know a man who can' is embedded in the DNA of a church that gathers disparate individuals and forms disciples in the name of Christ. The Church becomes a microcosm of the local area and the best place to establish a vision of what is needed for the well-being of the community.

An indication of maturity in discipleship is the habit of generosity. It builds up our shared life by transforming our habits of belief from an individual projection into a shared enterprise. How are we able to support communities of trust and love that show what kind of life is possible for those who believe that God is sovereign?

Wells (2006) writes that our common life is built up by friendship, finance and fun. The Sabbath puts money into perspective. In commercial terms everything must be paid for while in theological terms grace can never be earned. God's giving to us precedes any decisions we make about how to use our money. Life itself is a gift from God; the Son is God's gift to the world (John 3.16) and the Christian virtues are gifts of the Spirit (Gal. 5.22).

Our relationship with a consumer culture

Emperor Constantine adopted Christianity as the official state religion of the Roman Empire. Christians were no longer persecuted; Sunday was declared an official holiday; Eusebius went so far as to write that those who opposed Constantine were in fact attacking the Church.

Augustine, two generations later, living in the last days of the Roman Empire, needed to continue to establish the case for Christianity while ensuring that the Christians were not blamed for all that was by then going wrong in Roman society. Augustine had to display sufficient commitment to the Roman state for the Christians to be seen as good citizens, but sufficient distance from the state so that the Emperor's adoption of Christianity as the formal state religion was not made a scapegoat for the collapse of the Empire.

In our society consumerism appropriates the Church, as did the imperial power under Emperor Constantine. Foucault (2006) writes that capitalism creates a normative truth against which all other perspectives are judged. The Church faces the same challenge now as then to keep herself sufficiently distanced from the assumptions of the society to be able to maintain a distinctive witness. Once a payment has been introduced, the relationship is governed by the assumptions of consumerism. Church halls become income generators. When someone pays a set hourly rate for the use of a church hall then, to them, it is simply a commercial transaction. The church is seen simply as the service provider responsible for ensuring that there is enough toilet paper, that the cleaning has been done, and that the keys are available. The 'slimming club' or the 'yoga class' doesn't sit there feeling grateful to the church for providing access to a community space. They wonder about whether they are getting value for money.

Churches secure a distinctive witness to Christ by providing a counter-narrative, without which people simply buy into the manufactured meanings attached to consumer goods. Internet and television advertising is the liturgy of consumerism – Harley-Davidson motorcycles symbolize personal freedom, Nike shoes suggest health and fitness. Churches embody particular traditions, practices and ways of understanding the world, in developing a vision for the well-being of the wider society. Christianity is a narrative of social justice as well as of personal transformation. It changes society as well as lives. Wallis (2013) talks of the notion of the 'common good' as a framework for a Christian faith lived out in our public life. Working across society for the good of all is an outworking of Jesus' rallying cry for the Kingdom of God (Luke 17.21).

The Church is a conversational partner in what makes up for the common good of society. Archbishops and bishops make her especially able to be so with a network of local churches each supporting the voice of the other. A web of Christ-centred and outward-looking churches is God's stamp on society. The subtle nature of God's reign is not about power, but about a relationship of love and care in which God is identified as being in league with the most vulnerable in society.

Reflection

The PCC draw my attention to the extra 4 per cent that the diocese asks the church to contribute. This could be money spent on outreach projects in the parish. After a long discussion the committee suggests that, instead of reluctantly agreeing to the extra 4 per cent, we should cheerfully offer an extra 10 per cent. I am amazed at their generosity. It is an important moment for the church.

The deanery figures are published and I receive a telephone call from the incumbent of a parish in the deanery, which cannot afford to pay its contribution to the diocese. She thanks me for the generosity of my church, which, as she sees it, means that her parish can continue its mission.

Prayer

Lord God, I thank you for enabling a common good through the common purse. Help me to grow as a disciple of your Son as I make wise decisions about the quota. Amen.

R

Religion with spirituality

Religious and spiritual

'Religion' is an abused and misused term, and churches have lost their nerve in describing themselves as 'religious'. People talk of themselves as being 'not religious' as a claim to authenticity. Why is this? Religion is when life with God gets interesting: you are brave enough to encounter God in a real human community. You dig deeply into a rich seam of Christian tradition and your life is shaped by a great cloud of witnesses (Heb. 12.1).

Describing oneself as being 'not religious' underestimates the value of the Church 'doing religion' in an integrated, welcoming and Christocentric manner. Being a part of a church community provides people with a moral uplift, purpose and endeavour, social support and connections. These come with relationships, liturgy and simple grace; therein is the distinctive imprint of the local church.

People describe themselves as 'spiritual but not religious' as if it were some kind of daring insight, unique to them, bold in its rebellion against the religious status quo. They talk about seeing God in a sunset as if the idea of God in nature is a fresh idea and not one written up in the Psalms and embedded in the Christian tradition. Being privately 'spiritual' but 'not religious' doesn't cut to the heart of our faith. There is nothing challenging in having deep thoughts all by oneself without engaging with a wider community.

There is a distinction to be drawn between 'religion' as an institutional term and 'religion' as a shared endeavour. The former is that of which people rightly choose to distance themselves. Frost and Hirsch (2003, p. 21) criticize institutional religion as a traditional Church that is a hierarchical, bureaucratic, top-down model of leadership.

Religion is a shared endeavour and an integral part of our walk with Christ. As soon as there is more than one person involved, then religion is in play. It acts out the social structure of the faith – every Christian is a limb or organ of the collective body, which is Christ (1 Cor. 12.12ff.). All Christians bonded together as parts of this body have a duty to worship regularly with fellow Christians (Heb. 10.25).

It is an act of overwhelming significance that Christ left a community, rather than a body of written work, to embody his message. Nurturing a Christ-centred and outward-looking congregation is the distinctive task of the parish priest:

> Conversion does not pertain merely to an individual's act of conviction and commitment; it moves the individual believer into the community of believers ... people live in a series of integrated relationships; it is therefore indicative of a false anthropology and sociology to divorce the spiritual or the social sphere from the material and the social (Bosch, 2006, pp. 117, 10).

Christianity is not a private or solitary religion. Christians have a duty to worship regularly with fellow-Christians, in addition to their private prayers. Spirituality begins in the pews. The Epistle to the Hebrews (10.25) urges its recipients not to neglect regular meeting for worship.

Spiritual but not religious

The argument for people being spiritual but not religious has been that while institutional religion continues to decline there is a space opening up for other forms of spirituality. This re-enchantment theory is sometimes referred to as the 'Spiritual Revolution Thesis' (Heelas and Woodhead, 2004).

While institutional religion (and here we are normally talking about church religion) continues to decline on all normal measures of attendance, membership, financial giving, and so on, there is a space opening up for other forms of spirituality: 'Indeed, spirituality and religion can here be seen as separate if related entities

– when one increases the other decreases' (Heelas and Woodhead, 2004, pp. 20–1).

There are significant reasons for not drawing definitive conclusions about people being spiritual but not religious on the basis of Heelas and Woodhead's (2004) particular study of alternative spiritualities in Kendal in the Lake District. The research indicated that only just over 1 per cent of those involved in 'New Age' beliefs were aged between 20 or 30. The spiritual revolution, in this research, showed it is an older person's activity – and an older woman's pursuit at that.

The 'Spiritual Revolution Thesis' posits a move from religious disenfranchisement towards alternative spiritualities, but not the reverse. People who describe themselves as spiritual but not religious know enough about organized religion to say that they find it dull and want to move away. There is no evidence that people motivated by an inherent spirituality want to move towards religion.

The idea that there might be a natural development from spiritual feelings into religious participation ignores the incomprehensibility, the oddness and almost embarrassing strangeness of the Word made flesh (John 1.1). The Psalms talk about the presence of God in nature, but awe and reverence are not words exclusive to belief and do not lead naturally to an understanding of Christ, who had no beauty or majesty to attract us to him and nothing in his appearance to make us desire him (Isa. 53.2).

'Spiritual but not religious' is an idea attractive to church strategists because it provides a rationale for mission. If, so the argument goes, people are instinctively drawn to God (spirituality) but put off by the Church's corporate identity (religion), then all one has to do is to make the latter accessible and the former becomes expressible. This assumption does not reflect the research of Collins-Mayo, Mayo and Nash (2010) who established benevolent indifference as the attitude shown to the Church by those without enough knowledge of her workings to have yet formed hard and fast opinions.

Other terms have drifted from their original meaning and have acquired a currency for which they were never intended. A 'churchless faith' was never intended to suggest that there is an inherent spirituality within people that will flourish apart from the Church. The term 'churchless faith' was originally coined by Jamieson (2002) to refer to people who leave the Church but maintain an active faith in Christ. It is a challenge to the Church to keep pace with people's desire for continued and deeper discipleship.

People being 'put off by the Church but drawn to Jesus' is a second phrase that is misrepresented. Archbishop Temple's original use of these words was a call for the Church to be its robust missionary self. It is not intended to downplay the role of the Church. Archbishop Temple described the Church as a co-operative society existing for the benefits of its non-members. Our God-driven task is to invite all people to begin a new life as members of Christ's earthly community.

The phrase was intended to draw attention to the danger of the Church becoming too introspective. When the phrase is taken too literally and applied too generally though, it is taken to suggest that people come to a faith in Christ without the mediating presence of the Church. Without the Church it is not Jesus to which people are drawn, but towards romanticized self-made notions of Jesus.

Why do people like to make a virtue out of seeing themselves as being as little like a Church as they are able? Making a commitment to Christ is not simply a question of a person's feelings, but of an engagement with a community of faith. When Jesus challenged the rich young ruler to sell all he had and give to the poor, he did not ask him to go off on his own but to join up with his followers (Mark 10.21).

It is the gathered congregation that gives substance to our belief. Our strength as the Church lies in our collective relationships in the name of Jesus Christ. Our uniqueness lies in the one true historical faith. Our mission is to draw others into the story and to embody this in how we live our lives, shaping ourselves round the needs of the most vulnerable because therein lies the face of Christ.

A disparate congregation formed from among local people is a microcosm of the wider area and the best place to establish a vision of what is needed for the well-being of the community. Hauerwas (1981) talks of the Church as a counter-cultural distinctive and separate community of belief, shaping out the reality of God's love in the world. The religious task for the parish priest is to nurture a community of people with character and virtues sufficient to the job of witnessing to God's truth in the world.

The importance of religion lies not just in what we feel about it, but also what we do because of it. If there were any truth to the argument that the UK is a post-Christian country then it would be society that was disadvantaged. Christianity is the story of a thousand small kindnesses. In many of our most disadvantaged communities it is the churches that provide warmth, food, friendship and support for those who have fallen on difficult times. I clear up the excrement left in the churchyard by those sleeping rough and consider it my privilege to do so. Churches provide debt counselling, marriage guidance, childcare, after-school clubs and food banks – or sometimes someone simply there to listen: 'Religion that God our Father accepts as pure and faultless is this: to look after orphans and widows in their distress and to keep oneself from being polluted by the world' (James 1.27).

Formative and transformative spirituality

There is also a distinction to be drawn between what Collins-Mayo, Mayo and Nash (2010) refer to as 'formative spirituality' and 'transformative spirituality'. The first is a broad understanding that sees spirituality as a fundamental potential within the human condition. It is a positive and meaning-filled worldview, but with a limited working knowledge of the Christian faith. Spirituality in this sense is implicit in many individual actions and experiences. This might be appreciation of the natural world or a painting; loving and delighting in family and friends; feeling passionate about a social or environmental cause; expressing one's identity, etc. However, these phenomena may either not be recognized by the individual as spiritual, or else the spiritual aspect of them may be of little consequence to the individual concerned. This is a 'formative spirituality' because it is inherent in the human condition.

'Transformative spirituality' is the task of religion and the responsibility of the Church. Spirituality and religion belong to each other. Religion without spirituality is dogmatism; spirituality without religion is sentimentality. Religion with spirituality is the essence of true worship. 'Transformative spirituality' involves a conscious and deliberate attempt to develop beyond 'formative spirituality' in order to touch the deeper reality of a transcendent God. 'Transformative spirituality' involves the individual in deliberate practices that aim to foster mindfulness of God and help to maintain a sense of connectedness. This spiritual mindfulness then has significance for the individual in so far as it permeates daily life, guides the person's decisions, and provides a continued appreciation of God.

Reflection

Religion is making an emotional comeback. For over two years the parish experiments with three distinct services with different cultural flavours, worship styles, and at different times on Sundays. There is a time of reflection to take stock of all that has been achieved. This involves reinstating the original one main parish meeting for a trial period of six months.

Watching everyone worship God on our first day together is a profound and powerful moment. Our time apart in separate services is leading to rediscovery of religion. A 7-year-old talks and laughs with a 90-year-old. I can see the judge chatting to a vagrant, an Afro-Caribbean pensioner joking with a student, and a lady who comes on crutches interacting with a doctor – no medical textbook in sight. People with different understandings of spirituality experience the joy of a religious reunion.

I convince the PCC to turn reinstatement into restoration. Six months become a glorious for ever. I learn about various different ways of worshipping God, but my fundamental realization is that the power of gathered diversity in Christ is true religion and is more important than simply providing for different tastes.

Prayer

Heavenly Father, help me through my rediscovery of religion to worship your Son our Lord and Messiah. Amen.

S

Sabbath

It is the Sabbath that keeps the Church rooted in creation and focused on redemption.

Creation rooted

The climax of the creation story is not the creation of mankind on the sixth day. It is God resting on the seventh day. The goal of creation is not more and more, but completion, rest and delight.

God used the example of his resting on the seventh day of creation to establish the principle of the Sabbath day of rest. One day out of every seven the Israelites were to rest from their work and to give the same day of rest to their servants and animals (Ex. 20.8–11; Deut. 5.12–15).

Wells (2006) writes that the Sabbath is the gift to the Church to shape her life round the idea of play – what is exuberant, whole-hearted, passionate and joyful against the economic, measured, logical, effective strategic. Play is underestimated as a theological category. Play is seen as an optional extra rather than an integral part of how we live our lives: 'Play is frequently overlooked as an irrelevant part of people's social worlds' (Malbon, 1999, p. 11).

Children play in order to learn and to practise the skills they will need later on in life. Adults play in order to express delight and to exercise their imagination. The gift of creation in us is our laughter. Laughter is a Sabbath to the soul. Laughter is egalitarian and subversive. In carnival terms, laughter is seen as subversion, reshaping the power structures in the way that people relate to one another.

Redemption focused

Brueggemann (2014) writes that the Sabbath is an act of subversion against the demands of a consumer society. Without the Sabbath it is the economically powerful who decide on the norm. The teaching about the Sabbath in Leviticus was a practical hedge against the inevitability of the stratification of wealth and power within human societies. The Sabbath laws protected the weak and vulnerable against exploitation.

There was first of all the seventh day of each week, which was the Sabbath. Animals and slaves would be refreshed (Ex. 23.12). Every seventh year was a sabbatical year when the land was to lie fallow (Lev.25.10). All Hebrews who had been enslaved for debt were released and the debt thereby cancelled. Every seven sabbatical years – in other words every 50 years – was the year of jubilee. All land was returned to its original owners, since it was against the law to buy and sell land in perpetuity.

Sabbath stories of refreshment and redemption are acted out week by week in the parish church and transform the base line for what is possible within society. People meet together in the name of Christ and because of this there is no reason for vulnerable groups within our society to be left isolated. The needs of old people lonely at home, disaffected young people, servicemen just out of the army, people just out of prison, for all of whom there is limited social provision, can begin to be met through the phalanx of local churches that meet across the country.

Jesus clashes with the Pharisees on Sabbath days

The Sabbath day in creation was when God rested and was simply himself. In describing himself as the Lord of the Sabbath Jesus is claiming to be the God of creation (Matt. 12.1–8; Mark 2.23–28; Luke 6.1–5).

In the Gospels the Sabbath draws out issues of contention between Jesus and the Pharisees. For the Pharisees a legalistic view of religion meant a doctrinaire view of the Sabbath. The Pharisees condemn Jesus for healing a woman on the Sabbath (Luke 13.10–17). Jesus' response to them is that they have lost a sense of perspective. The Pharisees wait to see whether Jesus will heal a man with a crippled hand (Luke 13.10–17; Mark 3.4–6). Jesus challenges them to embrace the spirit of the Sabbath and to be less dogmatic about its application: 'Then he said to them, "The Sabbath was made for man, not man for the Sabbath"' (Mark 2.27).

Jesus commends David for eating the consecrated bread when his men are hungry (Matt. 12.1–8). Jesus escapes criticism twice for healing on the Sabbath – presumably because there were no Pharisees present (Mark 1.21–28; Luke 4.3–37).

Society's attitude towards the Sabbath

In our 24/7 cultures it is the Commandment both most needed and most easily ignored.

The Sabbath is the day on which the incongruity between a Christian worldview and that of a consumerist society is most especially marked. The Sabbath offers a trenchant criticism of an impatient and unforgiving age.

Society's attitude to the Sabbath is a marker for how we view the rest of our lives. For a twenty-first-century Christian, an intermittent approach to the Sabbath is a sign of the individualism that underpins modern-day society. Taylor (1992) writes that the price of individualism is a loss of purpose because we no longer have a bigger picture of events; everything is judged simply on the basis of how it affects *me*.

Our approach to the Sabbath is making a statement about what we consider to be important in the rest of our lives. There is no such thing as doing nothing – each action or inaction is a statement either condoning or disagreeing with what is being said or done around us. Without a Sabbath (Ex. 20.8) we remain a part of the set of attitudes that have governed the rest of our week and a market-driven social ideology rules unchecked.

Choice is a state of mind. With the rationale of a market economy as our de facto mindset, any claim on people's time becomes jumbled up with competing claims for their attention. Even church attendance becomes just one among a variety of options for how people can spend their Sunday mornings. Soccer matches invade our Sundays with parents on the touchline watching their children play, largely contained in market ideology, not wanting their children to miss out, and thinking of themselves as helpless before the requirements of such a commitment.

We start a half-hour service for football families on a Saturday evening. Children and their families are able to come to church, be home in time for tea, and then able to play football on Sunday morning. People now not only choose the church to which they want to belong, but also come to the service that suits them best. Consumerism brooks no dissent in its colonization of how to view the world.

What marks a modern-day Sabbath is the act of people coming together. A day off from work or time spent at home can be spent on one's own, whereas a Sabbath day is spent in the company of others. The Sabbath is my day of delight. It is the Sabbath time that I fritter away with the people that I love, the God that I worship, or the sport that I enjoy that takes me to the heart of the God I serve. A day off reinforces the importance of the working week because all I have to do is to get ready for the next one. My Sabbath gives me a glimpse of another way of life in which time is to be enjoyed, not used; a gift rather than a right, is God's time rather than my own.

Memory and faith

The Sabbath teaches us that time belongs to God (Ex. 20.8) in the same way that tithing teaches us that money belongs to God. The central command of the Sabbath is to remember (Ex. 20.8). We are an impatient and unforgiving society because we have lost the art of remembering well. There is no need for us to hold on to information because in a Wikipedia age there is always more information at hand. Forgetful of our past, we lose confidence in the future and grab at what is happening now.

Memory and faith run together. The foundation of Zechariah's new hope in Christ is the memory of God's covenant made with Abraham (Luke 1.72). The Church's Sunday by Sunday telling of the Christian story is an exercise in bringing to life the transformative memory of what God has done in Christ. The

Church is the original exponent of going 'Back to the Future'. Clergy are subversive traditionalists turning history on its head and bringing the story of salvation into the immediate present. The re-enacted memory of Christ's death and resurrection provides a critical standing ground for people's imagination. Christianity is a history with a future.

The evangelical call of the Sabbath is that it invites people to move beyond their individual frame of reference and to be a part of a wider story than just their own. The Sabbath is an exercise of collective imagination:

'If you keep your feet from breaking the Sabbath
and from doing as you please on my holy day,
if you call the Sabbath a delight
and the LORD's holy day honourable,
and if you honour it by not going your own way
and not doing as you please or speaking idle words,
then you will find your joy in the LORD,
and I will cause you to ride in triumph on the heights of the
    land
and to feast on the inheritance of your father Jacob.'
For the mouth of the LORD has spoken (Isa. 58.13–14).

Sabbath in the parish

The Sabbath is nowhere more readily ignored than in a parish church. It is in the nature of religious instruction that people need to be taught when they are most available: 'Every Sabbath he [Paul] reasoned in the synagogue trying to persuade Jews and Greeks' (Acts 18.4)

The irony for the clergy is that making the Sabbath day special for others, it is lost as such for them. They work on a Sunday when others have the time to meet, listen and come to church. For the best of motives, clergy have to professionalize their Sabbaths and act as if it were the sixth day of creation when there was still more to be done, rather than the seventh day when God rested from the work of creating the world (Gen. 1.31; 2.1).

My Sundays are hard work. I have responsibility for two different churches, half a mile apart, one of which begins an hour after the other. I run from one to the other so that I can be there for the start of the second service and spend as much time as I am able with each church.

Reflection

My preaching is shaped by my observation of the Sabbath. A rhythm of rest in the week helps me to pause in sermons. My pastoral work is more finely tuned if I have taken the Sabbath to listen to myself and to God; I listen to others better as a result. In pastoral conversations what people don't say is just as important as what they do say and I hear the silences better for having taken a day of rest. A practice of stopping in the week helps me to show people that a life of faith is a question of character rather than ethics. It is who I am rather than what I do that makes me a disciple of Christ. I serve the Lord better by observing the Sabbath than I would ever do by working seven days a week.

Prayer

Lord of the Sabbath, teach me to rest with intention and celebration, not when tiredness simply overcomes me. Amen.

T

Time

The Church is both a part of the establishment but also revolutionary. She has a social position at the centre of the community and a theological vocation to the edges. These roles are temporal and eschatological. Temporal time in the Bible is the Greek word *chronos*. Eschatological time is *kairos* – here is an example of each: 'When Jesus saw him lying there and learned that he had been in this condition for a long time [*chronos*]' (John 5.6).

Chronos is the measurable passage of time reckoned in a linear fashion: minutes, hours, days, weeks, etc. *Kairos* is the opportune moment in the day when a decision has to be made, insights are given, and realization comes. We are to: 'Be very careful, then, how [we] live – not as unwise but as wise, making the most of every opportunity [*kairos*], because the days are evil' (Eph. 5.15–16).

The challenge for the Church is to ensure that a diligence towards *chronos* time does not prevent us being ready for *kairos* moments. We tend to think of our time in a *chronos* mindset. We talk of having 24 hours in a day; we define our weeks by the number of hours that we work; we have a number of jobs to achieve in a day. We talk about being busy and not having time to do things without accepting that the time was never ours to not have in the first place.

Appreciating time eschatologically needs a mind shift away from an approach that treats time simply as an asset to be used, as we are best able. In Scripture, the Day of the Lord is subversion and not a calculation of *chronos* time. Eschatology is an understanding of the reality in which we live; it is not a speculation over some unspecified time in the future. In the Lord's Prayer we pray 'your kingdom come' as a recognition that time is not our own. Acceptance that time is not my own is acted out in microcosm when, for example, someone has a conversation that can't be postponed. They need to talk then, at that particular *kairos* moment.

A willingness to make one's time available to others is an integral part of the minister's role in the community. Conversations take time. Like the scattering of the seed, some will grow and multiply and others fade away (Mark 4.8). People want their minister to work hard, but they don't want her to be too busy to see people. The fact that people want their minister to be un-hurried and available to those in need is a gilt-edged invitation to the Church to be counter-cultural and different to the time-poor, relationship-squeezed society of which we are a part. Clergy are paid a stipend rather than a wage specifically so that they can have time for others.

Clergy are like the Little Prince in the fable, who lives on a small planet with three volcanoes and one plant (Saint-Exupéry, 1975). He travels from his planet and finds that people (grown ups) are involved in matters of great consequence, but actually there is nothing so important as him tending his rose plant back on his own planet. He meets a fox who explains to him why this is so: 'It is the time that you have wasted on your rose that makes your rose so important . . . It is only with the heart that one can see rightly, what is essential is invisible to the eye' (Saint-Exupéry, 1975, pp. 70 and 68).

Relationships take time. Jesus echoed the traditional clergy role of taking time visiting people in their homes. This is highlighted particularly in Luke (5.29, 7.36, 10.38, 11.37, 14.1, 19.5). Jesus visited rather than hosted because he had no home of his own to which he could invite people. The power dynamic in a home visit changes from priest to parishioner. The nomenclature for a church minister who has visited someone in their home changes from 'the vicar' to 'our vicar'. Home visiting is a time-consuming 'schmoozer' role. Putnam (2000, p. 93) describes those who spend many hours in informal conversation as *schmoozers*. Men and women who invest a lot of time in formal organizations are called *machers*. Both are different types of social capital.

Managing a parish takes time. A well-managed PCC needs a judicious balance between *kairos* and *chronos* time. *Kairos* is the opportune moment in the meeting when a decision has to be made, insights are given, and realization comes. *Chronos* has to be allowed for *kairos* insights to be reached.

Putnam (2000) describes social capital as the connections and relationships among groups and individuals. These are the social networks and the norms of reciprocity and trustworthiness that arise from them. Social capital is a specialism of a parish church. Faith communities are the single most important repositories of social capital. Regular church attendees reported talking with 40 per cent more people in the course of the day.

Being a schmoozer-priest is akin to being self-employed, or a housewife (or househusband), fairly able to set one's own schedule for the week. There is a recurring danger of unnecessary busyness. Clergy work on a Sunday and at (what are called) unsocial hours when others are home from work. They are already seen as a part of a 24/7 society. People see them as always working and assume that they are always busy.

Working too hard leaves clergy feeling isolated. We recognize the need to show an openhanded love and consideration to others. We are not so good at extending the same courtesy to ourselves. We are in the dreams business, helping people to become the person they have inside them to become. This requires creativity, care and imagination, and these aren't going to happen if we don't look after ourselves and instead end up feeling washed out and exhausted. 'Time off' is an issue for the clergy who are simply worn out, whether they know it for themselves or not. One of the things that many clergy opt not to do is take a day off. Hard-working clergy are driven by the idea that there is always more work to do than there are people to do it: 'The harvest is plentiful but the workers are few' (Matt. 9.37).

Working too hard becomes doctrinally embedded in the clergy's use of time when they do not give a proper weighting given to creation and eschatology in their teaching, reading and reflection. Grace becomes duty when preaching stops at the ascension. The congregation feels as if they are being asked to live up to the example of Jesus who lived, died and rose again 2,000 years ago rather than looking forward to his return. The fact that God redeemed the world through Jesus Christ becomes a challenge rather than a promise – we deny ourselves to follow Jesus (Mark 8.34); much is expected from people to whom much is given (Matt. 13.12).

'Redemptionitis'

At the end of a 70-hour working week I coin the phrase 'redemptionitis' to refer to what happens when *kairos* moments are swamped by the demands of *chronos* time and grace is lost to duty. Redemptionitis sermons are appealing – people would not otherwise get drawn into the trap of church busyness. They offer teaching that is clear and direct. They offer security, order and purpose and ask for morality, hard work and commitment in return. The focus is on action rather than on reflection. The story of what Jesus has done is treated as a challenge to us to go and live up to the exacting standards he has set, rather than an opportunity to celebrate and to enjoy the grace spaces that he has opened up.

Redemptionitis sermons are inspiring. They concentrate on Jesus' sacrifice and then challenge people to think what they might do in response. There is a need to 'press on towards the goal' (Phil. 3.14); we are the athlete in training (1 Cor. 9.25); we are the hard-working farmer who is the first to receive a share of the crops (2 Tim. 3.5). Under the guise of being obedient to God we are urged to do something to demonstrate our faith – be hot, be cold but just don't be lukewarm (Rev. 3.15); the only way not to be lukewarm, we are told, is to do something – what good is faith without deeds after all (James 2.14)?

Redemptionitis is a call for commitment. Christians are subdivided and then reclassified according to their levels of commitment – there are cultural Christians, believing Christians, born-again Christians, and then finally committed, Bible-believing, born-again Christians. The closer we get to the Church's centre the busier we become. The more we are drawn into church life, the greater is the compulsion put on us to live up to a theological ideal.

Redemptionitis sets the task of the Church in opposition to the redemption of unbelievers – as busy believers without the time or energy to talk to people about the faith, we strangle the message we claim to represent. As did the teachers of the law and the Pharisees, we shut the door of the kingdom of heaven in people's faces (Matt. 23.13). Activity-driven churches provide examples of *kairos* lost to *chronos*. If it is our behaviour rather than our belief that authenticates the gospel, then the pressure is on us to get things right:

> I can never be so confident of the authenticity of my witness that I can know that the person who rejects my witness has rejected Jesus. I am witness to him who is both utterly holy and utterly gracious. His holiness and his grace are as far above my comprehension as they are above that of my hearer (Newbigin, 1982, p. 151).

A proper weighting to grace comes with understanding that *chronos* will be subsumed into *kairos* as Jesus comes again to earth. Bosch (2003) writes that creation and redemption together offer reconciliation and grace. The incarnation was a part of God's original plan of creation, to be brought to fulfilment in the Second Coming of Christ. If Adam had not sinned, the Word would still have wanted to come to earth to enjoy fellowship with humanity.

Everything will pass away (Rev. 21) and we do not know when that will be (Luke 12.39). We must learn to live in the present moment and take each day as it comes (Matt. 8.20). When Jesus talked about faith the size of a mustard seed being able to move mountains (Matt. 17.20), he was not suggesting that we get out our spades and start digging. Ephesians presents the Church as God's masterpiece of reconciliation and a pilot scheme for the redeemed universe; however, this is a work of grace and not of effort and energy.

Reflection

Esther is a recent Christian who makes a request for me to visit her and her husband to talk about their growing faith. I ring and make an appointment, little knowing how important a *kairos* moment my visit will be, for myself as well as for her.

I enter the run-down estate, wary of barking dogs, fragmenting concrete and the unfriendly boarding on the windows of what seems to be every second house. I pray, as I do when approaching every home visit, asking for God's peace upon this place. Esther welcomes me at her door with a humble smile and I walk inside, instantly aware of a striking sense of calm and warmth in her flat.

As I am shown to the sofa, her husband is unable to stand to greet me: he has AIDS from the use of a contaminated needle and has weeks to live. Esther leads the discussion and talks steadily, but excitedly, about the experience of transformation by Jesus Christ in their lives over the past months. Death is coming to this family, but, she assures me, there is much to look forward to and a great deal for which to give thanks.

Prayer

Lord God, teach me about the balance of *chronos* and *kairos* in my life for your Son's sake. Help me to be a channel of your peace, rather than my programmes. Amen.

U

Understanding the role (disciple)

A Christian minister's vocation is to be a disciple of Christ. A disciple has the grace to share the space, and go at the pace of the other person. As with Philip and the Ethiopian eunuch (Acts 8.30), it is a calling to get alongside people and to listen to them before saying anything in return. The skill of a Christian minister is to see the world through other people's eyes. The role is that of an intuitive accompanier.

At one end of the age spectrum, I sit on a hospital bed with a lady who has recently had her 95th birthday and is telling me that she is lonely. At the other end of the age spectrum, I go on a train with a child the day before term starts in order to practise with him the journey into his new school.

A part of the church minister's role is to act as a *flaneur* (as he was known) in Paris in the nineteenth century. The word *flaneur* means a rambler, stroller, leisurely walker or promenader. Dr Stephen Roberts talked about how in the 1840s in Paris it was briefly fashionable to take turtles for walks in the arcades. The *flaneur* would walk at the pace of the turtle. Taking his pace from the turtle meant that the *flaneur* had the opportunity to stand apart from the crowd, time to walk slowly, and the chance to observe all that was happening. The parish priest, like the *flaneur*, is not in post to be busy but is there to walk slowly and to have time for people.

In a nursing home I sit for half an hour waiting for an older man finally to lift a glass of beer to his lips. The endless detail of people's lives demands constant attention. The minutiae of every-day living are the building blocks for the kingdom of heaven – not even a sparrow will fall to the ground apart from the will of the father (Matt. 10.29).

Building relationships across different social groups is creative, contextual and counter-cultural. I spend time at a football training ground. I make connections with the players once I start to wear a tracksuit and feel fully comfortable in their surroundings – we become all things to all people so that by all possible means we might save some (1 Cor. 9.20).

The process of accompanying, mentoring and befriending others is the way in which a minister acts out his vocation as a disciple. A church leader is both a disciple of Christ and a discipler of others. This is spelt out in the Great Commission:

> Then Jesus came to them and said, 'All authority in heaven and on earth has been given to me. Therefore go and make disciples of all nations, baptising them in the name of the Father and of the Son and of the Holy Spirit, and teaching them to obey everything I have commanded you. And surely I am with you always, to the very end of the age' (Matt. 28.18–20).

Jesus did not say 'make the world a better place' but go and bear witness to my name; making disciples is the means thereof. Making disciples is a verb. Teaching and baptizing are adverbs describing the process. We are called to be and to become a community of mission-focused disciples. A disciple is not a servant. Jesus calls us his friends and a friend is not a servant (see John 15.15): 'In a partnership, one does not serve because one is a servant. One serves because one is not a servant. And that service is much more meaningful and treasured precisely because it is not the service of servants but the service of equals' (Fung, 2002, p. 35).

A disciple's ministry is not incarnational. The term 'incarnational' is an unhelpful category for mission because it puts the emphasis on the messenger rather than the message and reflects society's individualism back on to itself. We domesticate the gospel by making it a lifestyle choice rather than the truth of Christ. Newell (2010) talks about the pious reader's habit of turning the gospel into a story about himself or herself: 'The pedagogues of piety rarely notice that they have turned the Gospel upside down; making should news out of good news' (Newell, 2010, p. 19).

If it is our behaviour rather than our beliefs that authenticate the gospel then the pressure is on us to get things right. When there are volunteers to be found, jobs to be done, and homes to be visited we feel that it is our fault if these things are not carried out. We feel that we are doing something wrong and make ourselves the scapegoat for declining numbers. Congregations are criticized for being too old, too few, or too set in their ways.

Schnabel (2005) writes that 'incarnational' is not a helpful theological category to describe the mission of the Church because the incarnation is a unique once and for all event (John 1.1) and not ours to carry on. The Christian finds the clue to the meaning of life in a particular historic event, unique, unrepeated and unrepeatable.

The nature of mission is described in Scripture as sending (John 20.21), serving (1 Cor. 9.19–23) and loving (John 13.34), but not incarnational. It is the nature of Jesus' relationship with his Father (Abba) (Mark 14.36) that we are asked to copy. The incarnational (John 1.14) manner of Jesus coming into the world is not a biblical template for mission.

The central activity for a disciple is to worship God and to help others to do the same. Mission is an attitude: churches have mission action plans or mission statements. Missions are events: people are sent out on missions. Missions are not the ultimate goal of the Church, worship is. God's purpose for the world is that 'the earth will be filled with the knowledge of the glory of the LORD as the waters cover the sea' (Hab. 2.14).

Worship uncovers, undermines, and even destroys anything that keeps people separate and apart from one another. Those who would otherwise be separated by economic, racial and social constraints come into free and familiar contact with one another. It is the activity of the Holy Spirit that makes the crowd into a community. The believing congregation is an extravagant juxtaposition of rich and poor, spiritual and material, young and old, male and female.

The multi-layered nature of truth is evident in a congregation. Truth is understood by some, but not by all. Disciples are given the secrets of the Kingdom of God, but to those on the outside everything is told in parables (Mark 4.11). Truth is hidden from the wise and intelligent and made known to infants (Matt. 11.25). A relationship with Christ is an indefinable work of the Holy Spirit (1 Cor. 12.3). It takes being drawn into a network of relationships within a church congregation to discover its true nature. Congregation members participate before they understand that of which they are becoming a part.

It takes an unpaid army of volunteers and a range of skills from the clergy to keep a parish church open. The core skills for a church minister are to be patient, thoughtful and organized – patience in order to be a pastor (Col. 3.12), thoughtful in order to be a teacher (James 3.1), and organized in order to be a steward of time and task (1 Cor. 4.2). To be a pastor without being a teacher is sentimentality. To be a teacher without being a pastor is dogmatism. To be a teacher and pastor together takes grace and judgement (Eph. 1.17). Newbigin (1982) underpins much of contemporary mission thinking. He highlighted the dangers of ghetto-ization:

> The first danger is that the Church may so conform its life and teaching to the culture, that it no longer functions as the bearer of God's judgment and promise. It becomes simply the guardian and guarantor of the culture and fails to challenge it. The next danger is that the language and lifestyle of the church should be such that they make no contact with the culture and become the language and lifestyle of a ghetto (Newbigin, 1986, p. 96).

People respond to the position I hold. They script me into roles that I am not aware I occupy in their minds. They are then angry or pleased according to how well or not I occupy that role. How I respond to people is how they respond to me. If I continually relate to someone therapeutically, he will eventually respond pathologically; if I ask enough times whether there is anything that I can do to help he will soon assume that there is something there that he needs to be helped with.

When Jesus goes into the Garden of Gethsemane he takes Peter and the two sons of Zebedee with him (Matt. 26.37). Judas has gone to the chief priests (Matt. 26.14). The remaining eight disciples are simply told to sit (Matt. 26.36) – the hour has come and there is nothing more for them to do. I have been a parish priest for ten years. If I had been one of the eight disciples left at the gate of the Garden of Gethsemane and told simply to sit, I would have found it hard. I would have wanted to arrange a rota for the eight of us and do something to help with the situation. I would have had to learn afresh that the heart of a disciple's role is a willingness to sit and to wait on God.

Reflection

Two members of our church run a boxing club as a parish activity in the church hall for teenagers on the margins. I discover the joy of being a volunteer when one of them cannot be there. There is no pressure on me to step in and they are surprised when I do. The leader is pleased to have me unexpectedly present. I am glad to have the chance to learn from him.

I watch and take note as he trains and builds up the young people: encouraging, laughing, instructing, scolding, guiding, and caring. The time comes for the boxers to leave and I stay behind to clear up with the leader. I thank him and say goodbye, turning to leave. He calls me back and suggests that we should end the evening in prayer. On this occasion it is I who am the disciple and he the disciple.

Prayer

Heavenly Father, thank you for the great privilege of being called to make disciples. Help me to delight in opportunities to learn from others as much as they may be glad to learn from me. Let me, as your disciple, serve the people of the parish as an equal in Jesus Christ. Amen.

V

Volunteer to disciple

Voluntarism and grace are at the heart of our faith. In voluntarily holding his divine nature in check and taking on the nature of a servant (Phil. 2.7), Jesus gave us a chance to respond freely to God's love. Jesus is reticent about the claims he makes for himself and in what he lets others say about him. The consequence of his tempered approach is that people are invited in to take part in his ministry. There are silences that are an expression of power. Jesus' silences are pauses for invitation (Isa. 53.7).

A church leader looks to create such a spirit of accompaniment in her work with volunteers. In Scripture she is described as working both for God (Eph. 6.5–9) and with God (2 Cor. 6.1). There is a parallel process in her work in the church. She is working for the church immediately after her arrival. Her initial stages in the post are a chance for her to establish a presence and bed in a vision for the church. She is honouring the relationships within the congregation and the plans for the future that are already in place. If this stage continues for too long, it leaves her feeling isolated – either excluded from the decision-making process or else under pressure to do everything herself. 'This is how we have always done things' is a phrase used to stifle mission initiative.

She is working with the church, if she is able, to establish a collaborative model of church leadership. People see themselves as working together in a common endeavour but are willing and ready to look to the church leader to set a direction. The congregation learns what is distinctive about the church leader and what in particular she has to offer.

A strong lay leadership willing to share responsibility for the running of the church is integral to church growth. This is reflected in the report *From Anecdote to Evidence: Findings from the Church Growth Research Programme (2011–2012)*. The report

(Archbishops' Council, 2014) identifies that churches where volunteers are involved in leadership, and where roles are rotated regularly, is likely to be growing – especially where younger members and new members are included in lay leadership and service.

A ladder of involvement helps to map these different stages of a relationship that people will have with the Church and to mark their process from volunteer to disciple:

1 The first rung of the ladder is 'awareness'

This is a low-level type of cultural engagement. In the 2011 Census 59 per cent of the population identified themselves as Christian. At the same time, Brierley (2014) reckoned that only 3.75 per cent (2.4 million) would have been in regular church attendance.

People take for granted the social role of the church to mark and manage life events (e.g. baptisms, weddings or funerals). Grace Davie (Davie, 2007) writes that in the historical parochial system the church is seen as a 'public utility' just like its parallels in health or welfare offering care at the point of need.

People make occasional visits to the church (e.g. Christmas, Easter, Remembrance Sunday). Beyond those occasional visits they are happy for others to believe and do what they want provided it is not imposed on them. There is still a natural wariness of having religion forced upon the self by others.

2 The second rung is 'interest'

This is a conscious low-level type of engagement with the church. It marks a transition from passive awareness to personal choice. Anyone motivated enough to get out of bed on a Sunday morning to come to church clearly wants something. This can vary from the need for comfort after the death of a loved one, an unspecified interest in the faith, or the need to attend regularly because they want a reference for a church school. People are variously described as 'seeker', 'consumer', 'spiritual searcher', 'enquirer'.

Exposure to a Christ-centred, outward-looking congregation leaves people intrigued. A believing, celebrating, loving Christian community fully invested in the life of the community will not be able to withhold from others the secret of its hope.

3 The third rung is 'involvement'

Coming to church is a choice, but staying in the church is a commitment. An attractive profile, a well-designed website or a good reputation in the community can get someone from 'awareness' to 'interest'. It is a commitment to Christ and relationships with others in the congregation that will get someone from 'interest' to 'involvement'. Involvement requires traction as people form friendships, identify with people with common interests, and come to feel that they belong. They appreciate the wider church community of which they have become a part. People used to come to church because it was a part of a community. Now people come to church to find a community.

Involvement may mean volunteering on a social action project run by the church. This can be participation in a church programme such as parent and toddler groups or provision for the elderly and homeless. A blending of gospel distinctiveness and social inclusivity is a natural position for a parish church wanting to be a microcosm of their local community. A strong-centred Church with soft edges allows for multiple points of access and leaves people able to find their own level of belonging. This is a blend of 'Christendom' and 'community' models of church. The former is a self-referential congregation, each responding to the other. The latter is an outward-focused congregation looking to draw others in.

Bob Jackson (Jackson, 2002) wrote that churches conducting few funerals were actually growing better than those still conducting many because the clergy were freer to concentrate on growing the gathered congregation. The church members largely do the community ministry and the clergy do the Christendom ministry. The connectedness to the local community depends more on the strength of the church than the ability or inclination of the clergy.

4 The final rung is 'ownership'

The final rung is 'ownership'. This is the stage at which people have become mature in the faith, attaining to the whole measure of the fullness of Christ (Eph. 4.13). People join committees, go to Small House Groups and take on responsibility for the life of the parish. The skill of a church minister is to ensure that people are both volunteers and disciples. The minister has to make sure that people's faith in Christ and commitment to the Church feed one another.

This mutuality reflects the clergy's own weekly balancing act. She has both to organize the logistics of running a church as well as lead people in worship. On the one hand, there is a photocopier or printer needed to prepare service sheets for Sunday. On the other hand, there are the relationships, prayer, Bible study and worship needed to build up a faith in Christ. To view the mission of the Church through the lens of volunteerism underplays the significance of discipleship, which is a life of obedience (Matt. 16.24).

The pull of volunteering swamps the claims of discipleship. Jobs needing to be done fall on a central group of volunteers. There is always more work to do than people to do it (Matt. 9.37). Maintenance issues for a church hall can swamp a church's volunteer capacity. Clergy rely on the commitment and good will of hard-working volunteers who make it their task to keep the church buildings open and in good order.

Rural vicars with responsibility for three or more congregations find that any sense of mission is squeezed by their responsibility for the church buildings. Volunteers who offer to mow the lawn or to clean the church are at a premium. People in their sixties and seventies are the new Marthas and Marys.

Volunteers become disciples through them forming collective relationships in the name of Jesus Christ. Our uniqueness lies in the one true historical faith. Our mission is to embody this in how we live our lives, shaping ourselves round the needs of the most vulnerable because therein lies the face of Christ.

The worship place is practice for the market place. People learn how to relate to those they might never have otherwise met and, in doing so, they find new ways of being in the world. People gather together, as a part of the process of community forming in and through the name of Christ. A church is simultaneously a gathering and sending community. It is both centripetal (drawn inwards) and centrifugal (thrown outwards) because each is a part of the other.

Newbigin (1989) talks of the local church as being sign, instrument and foretaste of God's redeeming grace. She is a sign pointing to a reality beyond the present horizon. She is an instrument used by God for his work of blessing. She is a foretaste because church is a place where people can have a first taste of the joy and freedom God intends for all. The fruit of the holy marriage between Christ and his Church is a new creation.

Volunteers become disciples through taking part in the Church's trinitarian expression of God. At church committee meetings people agree on the priorities, decide on jobs, and ask for volunteers. An agreement reached illustrates the unity of the Spirit through the bond of peace (Eph. 4.3). The work of the Holy Spirit is to create unity in diversity rather than harmony in similarity. The jobs that need to be done to ensure that the church stays open keep alive the collective story of God the Father's love. The volunteers embody the story and reflect the obedience shown by Jesus (Rom. 5.19).

Being made in the image of God does not mean individual enlightenment, but rather community learning. Genz (2001) argues that the image of God is a social rather than an individual reality – it is a way of relating to other people rather than the idea that there is a spark of light hidden deep within us. The biblical focus is on 'we' being the divine image rather than the image being lodged within each individual. The *imago dei* is a communal concept. The locus of the divine image in the New Testament is the community of Christ rather than the individual believer. The Church is not a free association of volunteers, but a group of disciples acting in obedience to the claims of the risen Lord.

Reflection

One woman, with a faith awaiting maturity, is frustrated by the lack of 'can-do' mentality when it comes to Sunday service hospitality. She takes on a significant role in order to make it function better and, as a result, becomes one of the most reliable prayer intercessors in the parish through her need to call on God's help for her new volunteering role. She climbs two rungs of the ladder − from 'interest' through 'involvement' to 'ownership'.

I see her discipleship becoming committed and marvel as it carries her through a very difficult relationship break-up. I know that her previous level of faith would not survive such trauma, but she has a new understanding of God's faithfulness through her volunteering. She tells me that the effort of serving as part of a team has led her to give God access to her daily life, so that she stands strong like a reinforced tower in the wind of personal pain. Soon, I observe others looking to her for inspiration in their own journey as Christian disciples.

Prayer

Lord God, thank you for this glorious vocation of volunteering my life as my response to your love for me in Christ Jesus. Help me to see the broad picture of your plan to draw people closer to you through the service of being volunteers in your Church. Amen.

W

Words

The generative power of words is shown in the creation account. Genesis does not indicate the creation of language, but instead shows the use of language as the creating power: 'In the beginning was the Word' (John 1.1) and 'God said, "Let there be light," and there was light' (Gen. 1.3).

Ezekiel (4.6) lay on his right side for 40 days, prophesying against a clay model of Jerusalem as a symbol of God's judgement against Judah. Isaiah (20.3) walked around naked 'and barefoot for three years', as a symbol of God's judgement on Egypt and Ethiopia. A Church of England vicar preaches once a week and is expected to bring Scripture to life.

Preaching is a technical skill as well as a theological imperative. I emphasize a point by a change in tone rather than by an increase in volume. I break down 'the fourth wall' to establish a rapport with the congregation. 'The fourth wall' is an expression stemming from the theatre. A room will consist of three physical walls, as well as an imaginary fourth that separates the world of the actors from that of the audience. I look at the congregation's foreheads (rather than the eyes) to maintain eye contact with all – focusing on the eyes of one person alone excludes the rest. I exercise a playfulness in my preaching since one of the implications of the parable of the sower is that most people are not going to understand what is being said anyhow.

Sermon preparation time is a regular casualty of a busy week in a parish. This is when exegesis becomes eisegesis. *Exegesis* (from the Greek *ex*, meaning *out of*) is the discipline of drawing out the meaning and spelling out the implications of Scripture. *Eisegesis* (from the Greek *eis*, meaning *into*) is a process of reading my own pre-set ideas into the text.

Exegesis becomes eisegesis when a sermon is shaped more by my thoughts about the text than the actual text itself. I have previous sermons that I can use again. An item of news, a story of what had happened during the week, could each be used to frame a sermon but still take attention away from the actual text. Personal stories provide illustrations, but are not in themselves explanations of a passage. Everyone loves a good story, but illustrations are no *substitute* for exegesis. An exegetical sermon takes longer than an eisegetical one to prepare. I count on half an hour's preparation time for every minute that I preach. A ten-minute sermon takes me five hours to prepare.

Scripture shows words and images used together. Dulles (2005) writes that the contemporary crisis of faith is a crisis of images. The provocative quality of image is deployed throughout Scripture. Elisha used a bow and arrow (2 Kings 3.15) and Ahijah (1 Kings 11.30) tore up his cloak to get his message across. Jeremiah used a variety of props to 'image' rather than verbalize his message. These included a loin-cloth (linen belt in the NIV) (13.1–14), pottery (8.1, 9.15), goblets of wine (25.15–36), stones (43.8–13), scrolls (51.62–64) and yokes (27.1, 28.17). Jesus used a child to illustrate the nature of the kingdom of heaven (Matt. 18.3), a fig tree to illustrate the nature of faith (Matt. 20.18), and a coin to illustrate the nature of good citizenship.

Words on the internet

Electronic media allow for a transfer of ideas, accessibility of information, and ease of communication. When God created the world his first category was time. He called the light 'day' and the darkness 'night' (Gen. 1.5). His second category was space. He separated the sea from the land (Gen. 1.9). His third category was people. He created humankind in his own image (Gen. 1.27). Electronic media bring together 'time', 'space' and 'people' into the single click of a button. I can log on to my computer in the morning and find out straight away who said what, where and when.

What the internet does not offer is a shared understanding of the common good. When everyone has the right to express an opinion and there is no context to what is being said, then there is no immediate way of deciding what is right or wrong. I 'unfriend' or I 'unlike' someone to withdraw approval. I 'LOL' (laugh out loud) or I think OMG (Oh my God). Who has the final authority to decide what is noble, right and pure (Phil. 4.9)? In the words of T. S. Eliot: 'Where is the Life we have lost in living? Where is the wisdom we have lost in knowledge? Where is the knowledge we have lost in information?'

Music, moving images and dialogue blend together in a cultural environment such as cinema, the internet and television. Running the three together mirrors the way that children and young people think. They do not rationalize conceptually in a linear and progressive manner. Ideas come in a random order demanding immediate attention – imagination, events, ideas and opinions run into one another. Multi-layered learning is their natural medium. In church music, images and dialogue will happen sequentially. We will listen to a sermon, stand to sing a hymn, turn to look at the stained glass windows.

Words in church

According to Macintyre (1990), one's understanding of what makes for the common good is decided by the primary community of which one is a part. For a Christian, this is a church. In the church context, learning is structured and words are carefully modulated. The church marks its theological territory by running the three popular artistic milieu (word, music, image) in sequence rather than simultaneously – a sermon (word) is followed by a hymn (music), which is followed by image (the bread and the wine).

The preaching of the Old Testament prophets is able more naturally to blend words with image or music. Ezekiel (Ezek. 37) prophesies to a valley full of dry human bones. The bones connect into human figures, become covered with tendon tissues, flesh and skin, and are then revealed as the People of Israel who would come to life and return to the Land of Israel.

The difference between church words and prophetic voices is that the latter were consciously taking their listeners beyond naturally held assumptions about their immediate world order. Isaiah foretold the coming of the Babylonian captivity (Isa. 39).

Jeremiah told them to accept the period of captivity as just punishment from God for their sins (Jer. 25). Ezekiel looked forward
to the return of the Israelites from Babylon to Jerusalem (Ezek.
20.39–44).

The prophet speaks into a situation. The priest speaks out of a
situation. The prophet represents God to man; the priest officiates
from man to God. Both stand on the boundary between earth and
the divine. Words are the tools of the prophet and priest. Words
reflect and connect with those who already have an understanding
of the Christian faith. Symbols and images are the tools of the
prophet. They encourage others to explore further. Words build
on how people already understand the world. Images and symbols
awake an interest in people, entice them to move beyond what
they already know, and to look at things in a new and different
way.

Words and silence

In church I use silences to help people to interact with what I have
been saying. People have the capacity to speak up to 125 words a
minute but the ability to listen to 400 words. This means that the
listener of a sermon is occupying only 30 per cent of their mind
and holding the other 70 per cent in check. Silences allow people
to ponder on what has been said and to translate the ideas of a
sermon into their own context.

Silences change a speech into a sermon and turn an audience
into a congregation. A speech is informational, while a sermon
is experiential, relational and transformational. An audience
is passive. A congregation is participative. Words provoke but
silence echoes. Words challenge but silence encourages. Silence is
a created space in which people are free to reflect and to respond
to what they are hearing being said. It is in the shared moments of
silence when words are most clearly heard. T. S. Eliot wrote that
the stillness for which the soul should strive is as 'when an underground train, in the tube, stops too long between stations and the
conversation rises and slowly fades into silence'.

Mark's Gospel uses silences to draw in people who would otherwise be marginal figures. Jesus is an enigmatic figure and silences

throw the emphasis on to the people he meets. The 'Messianic Secret' is the term used to refer to the repeated instances in which Jesus is portrayed as commanding his followers to silence. He told the healed leper to tell no one what had happened (Matt. 8.4). He drove out many demons, but he would not let the demons speak because they knew who he was (Mark 1.34).

As a literary device, the Messianic Secret draws the readers into the telling of the story by requiring them to come to conclusions about Jesus themselves without Mark spelling it out for them. Mark's Gospel was not written until a generation after Jesus' death. The story of Jesus' life had been passed on by word of mouth, and so the truth of his divine identity would have been known within the early Church. The Gospel reader feels 'in on the joke', as they read of how the events unfolded rather than have their reaction dictated.

Brueggemann (1989) writes that the artistry of the preacher is to disclose the power of guilt and of healing and to lead the congregation through the delicate transaction whereby healing overcomes and overrides guilt. The mandate of the preacher is to take people from confession through to worship, from Adam to Christ, from sin to grace.

Jesus is the master craftsman in the art of sermon delivery. Lewis and Lewis (1983) write that in the Sermon on the Mount Jesus asks 19 different questions. He gives six contrasts between the old teachings of the Torah and his own new teaching. There are four different types of teaching shown by Jesus, all of which might blend together in a single sermon. As I preach I am illustrating, explaining, challenging and encouraging people to respond to the claims of the living God:

a) Illustrate (homilia)

'What is the kingdom of love like? What shall I compare it to? It is like a mustard seed' (Luke 13.18–19).

Jesus made illustrative comparisons to tell stories, capture people's imagination, and to draw people in to engage them with his teaching. This is the art of apologetics. Apologetics is the theological discipline that concerns itself with how the gospel should be presented, mindful of the particular culture and context in which this is to happen.

b) Explain (exegesis)

He did not say anything to them without using a parable. But when he was alone with his own disciples, he explained everything (Mark 4.34).

Jesus was reinterpreting the Old Testament, and so taking time to explain to his disciples what he was doing provided critical hinge points to his ministry. This is the art of exegesis and is the gift that the preacher gives to modern-day disciples motivated enough to be in church sitting and listening. Exegesis provides a context-based critical reflection, an explanation of the meaning of Scripture: read a passage through, dig it up, pray it in, and live it out. The heart of my Sunday preaching is not what I think of the passage, but what the passage says of itself.

c) Challenge (exousia)

[Jesus] taught as one who had authority, and not as their teachers of the law (Matt. 7.29).

The Jews grumble at Jesus because he calls himself the bread that came down from heaven. Jesus reiterates his claim to authority by describing himself as the 'bread of life' (John 6.48). Evangelism has a wider currency than simply one person asking another to commit their life to Christ. Evangelism is the process whereby people are confronted with the claims of the living God and are encouraged to respond collectively.

d) Encourage (paraklesis)

Jesus told his disciples a parable to show them that they should always pray and not give up (Luke 18.1).

I preach first to myself and so, in encouraging others from the pulpit, I am drawing them in to my own life of discipleship.

Reflection

How can I talk so that people listen, and listen so that people will talk? How do I know when to pause and to leave spaces rather than rushing to fill silence with words? I receive as much positive feedback when I create time for reflection, as I do from sermons with a great turn of phrase.

It is satisfying to watch people's faces when I give my Sunday sermon. It is fulfilling to hear a person's tone change from sadness to hope, because I give time for people to sit in silence and to listen together.

I need the wisdom of the Holy Spirit to know when to talk and when to keep quiet. I need always to be quick to listen and slow to speak (James 1.19). I know that on every occasion I open my mouth I am one step away from either giving glory to God or else attracting attention to myself.

Prayer

Lord God, thank you for the honour of being able to use words as a blessing to others. Help me to honour you through language, and silences, music and image, virtual reality and daily living. Amen.

X

Christmas

We have a carol service for children with special needs. It is a wonderful occasion. The children doing the Bible readings work their way slowly through each of the words in the passage, but no one in the congregation seems to mind. One of the children has Down's syndrome and shares the reading of the Gospel passage with her brothers. It is lovely to have children at the centre of the service and not to have their parents needing to keep them quiet so that they don't disturb everyone else.

After the service I talk with a mother and kneel to make eye contact with her child. He takes my head in his hands and sucks my nose. It is a tender moment, with him taking the lead and pleased at what he is doing. I am tentative and unsure of myself but do not stop him. He continues for a while. He is going to spend the rest of his life on the edge of other people's conversations, and so for that moment I feel that he can do as he wishes. I feel very fortunate.

The child is my lodestar for the Christmas season. We, in the Church, find it easy to bemoan the effects of a consumerist culture on our Christmas celebrations. The greatest single knock-out blow delivered to Christianity by a consumerist culture is to see Christmas replace Easter as the main festival of the Christian year. Some 3.7 million people are reckoned to have logged on for the online Christmas sales (2013) that began at 12.01 a.m. on Christmas Day, while only 2.5 million go to church later on in the day. It is thought that 66 per cent of the population will be asleep at 4 p.m. on Christmas Day. This all means that the Church is operating in a crowded market in trying to make 25 December its one showcase day to get its message across. The story is told as if it all happens within a 24-hour period: Mary and Joseph arrive;

a stable is found; the baby is born; the shepherds and wise men visit.

The real tragedy is not so much that the Christmas message has been taken from us but that we have given it away. The Church offers to society a theology that is more 'Away in a manger' with the little Lord Jesus' sweet head than 'Hark the herald angels sing' along with the second person of the Trinity. Jesus was defenceless but he was not helpless.

In Scripture Jesus is no longer a newborn infant when the wise men arrive. They don't come to Bethlehem until some time after Jesus' birth. They arrive at a house, rather than a stable, and see Jesus as a young child rather than as a baby (Matt. 2.11). Herod wanted all children under two to be killed, an intimation of the future suffering that lay ahead for this young child.

It is natural that we interpret the baby Jesus through the lenses of childhood with which we are most familiar. Modern notions of childhood touch on vulnerability and need. This is encapsulated in pictures of the baby Jesus cosseted and protected in pristine clean stable stalls. Childhood is to be nurtured and protected: it is age-graded and a gradual progress towards adulthood.

The idea that Jesus had to grow gradually into an awareness of his divine status appeals to contemporary notions of authenticity and self-realization but it has a pre-trinitarian logic of Jesus as subordinate rather than co-equal with God as Father and Holy Spirit. It is not a notion of childhood that can be mapped on to Jesus who was God in the womb (Luke 1.31, 35). God chose the time (Gal. 4.4) and the place (Micah 5.1) for his birth. The baby Jesus would have been akin to the disabled child who sucked my nose. He would have had a clear sense of who he was as the world changed around him.

Once, as I was cycling home, two young people sped past me on their bicycles. One of them turned round and shouted 'Get an upgrade!' It is maybe this that the Church needs for its Christmas message. I like to finish my Christmas Day sermon with the notices for Easter. We preach Christ crucified (1 Cor. 1.23), not Jesus lying in a manger, even if in our Christmas-Christianity it has become the latter. It is correct that in Jesus' story we run together his birth and death. When Jesus is presented in the temple, Simeon tells Mary a sword will pierce her soul (Luke 2.35).

John Stott (2006, p. 24) describes Jesus as born in the shadow of the cross.

On Christmas Day we see the trajectory of God's character stretched across eternity – the pre-existent Word has become the living man (John 1.14) and will come as the returning King (Rev. 3.21). Jesus' birth in Bethlehem was T. S. Eliot's still point of the turning world where past and future are gathered together: in the beginning of the story lies its end. We announce to people that the world has changed and we rejoice.

The four weeks of Advent are intended as the Church's time of preparation after which the celebrations finally begin. The angels 'hark' only when the baby Jesus is born and they have something to 'hark' about. In liturgical terms, the 12 days of Christmas start on 25 December and end on 5 January with the Feast of the Epiphany during which our joyful celebrations continue.

When the Church reverts to a pious approach in an attempt to claim back the Christmas story, we talk about 'the true meaning of Christmas' as if we can appreciate it and *others* can't. T-shirts with 'Happy birthday, Jesus' or 'Don't forget the reason for the season' dictate a response, but make light of the depth of meaning for our lives.

In the culture of consumption of which we are a part, people who may not have been in church from one year to the next will still want a traditional Christmas carol service available on demand. The Church acts more as a service provider than a truth teller. At Christmas the local church is seen as the guardian of a cultural heritage rather than a community of faith.

Nativity plays and carol services cherish people's lost ideal of a family narrative rather than challenge them to live a new life in Christ. One year I had a nativity scene with neither a Mary nor a Joseph. She had not appeared and he refused to go on stage because he had wanted to play the role of an innkeeper. People were charmed because the appeal of nativity plays and carol services are driven more by a nostalgia for childhood than by any desire from them to learn the true meaning of Christmas.

However, the happy family narrative is divisive. At Christmas people feel excluded if they don't have a family group to join and are sometimes pressurized if they do. Research from Age UK in 2014 concluded that 23 per cent of those aged over 65, the equivalent of 2.5 million people in Britain, do not look forward to Christmas because of loneliness and the fear that it will bring back bad memories.

Christmas cards used to be about mangers, kings and shepherds. Then they became about reindeer and robins. Now they are about us, ourselves. We send out Christmas newsletters telling others of what we have done during the year. There are even Advent calendars that go up to New Year's Eve and New Year's Day and thus script out the significance of Christmas Day itself. As the cultural memory of Christianity fades, people are left to respond to the gospel individually and on the basis of what it means to them. We can't call people to repent because Christmas is near, because there is no common understanding of Christmas as there would have been a common understanding of the kingdom of heaven when John the Baptist preached.

There are different worldviews in play. At our carol services we present the Christian story within one framework of interpretation, but it is listened to within another. We read the nine lessons, give out Alpha leaflets, sing carols and pray. People eat mince pies, drink mulled wine, and enjoy the festive cheer that marks the beginning of their holiday season.

Santa Claus is the public face of Christmas-Christianity. I have my annual conundrum of whether it matters my being Father Christmas at the school fete one week and then vicar in church the next. The same children will be sitting on my knee telling me what they want for Christmas one day and then hearing me preach in church on another.

C. S. Lewis gives a hint as to how Santa Claus might best be included in our Christmas celebrations by writing him into *The Lion, The Witch and The Wardrobe*. Father Christmas's appearance in Narnia seems incongruous because there is no mention made otherwise either of Christ or of Christmas. Father Christmas comes just as the spell of the White Witch begins to weaken. The snow starts to melt and he arrives with sleigh bells jingling. He is 'a huge man in a bright red robe (bright as holly berries) with a hood that had fur inside it and a great white beard that fell like a foamy waterfall over his chest'. C. S. Lewis is here reclaiming Christmas as a celebration that is forward-looking and outward-reaching. The children receive presents, but they are tools that they will need to use in the near future to bring about the downfall of the wicked White Witch. Peter is given a shield and a sword. Susan is given a quiver full of arrows and a little ivory horn to call for help. Lucy is given a little glass bottle of healing cordial and a small dagger to defend herself. C. S. Lewis is redeeming the role of Father Christmas because his appearance in Narnia is forward-looking and apocalyptic, helping the children to prepare for the coming battle with the wicked queen.

The Christmas festival is a hope for the future. It is a love affair between God and mankind. If things were so different in the past when Jesus was born in Bethlehem they can be so again in the future when Jesus returns to earth. The eschatological hope of Christmas is evident within some of the carols we already sing. We can truly rejoice through the realization that the tiny infant Jesus is God himself, who has come to share our lives and to save us from ourselves. As the words of the carol say:

Hail, thou ever-blessed morn!
Hail, redemption's happy dawn!
Sing through all Jerusalem,
Christ is born in Bethlehem!
Lo, within a manger lies
He who built the starry skies;
He who, throned in height sublime,
Sits amid the cherubim.

Reflection

The only quiet moment I am able to grab in the run-up to Christmas turns out to be among the most profound I have. I walk into church alone and sit down five rows from the front, feeling enchanted by the silence. As I begin to pray, my eyes are open and they settle on the Christmas tree, which has been beautifully decorated the previous day. There is a subtle glow from the minute lights, but more conspicuous is the perfect arrangement of equidistant blood-red bows, neatly tied and spaced, contrasting tastefully with the deep-green pine branches.

I know that the Christmas tree originates from Germany. The living pine in winter brings to mind the birth of Christ. The triangular shape points to heaven. These red bows give rise to a time of prayer for me in which I absorb the eschatology of Christmas. I envisage the tree upon which Jesus hung, with his blood dripping in volumes for me. I find myself reciting 'Christ has died, Christ is risen, Christ will come again.'

My Christmas addresses are going to take on a renewed sense of passion due to my silent moment alone in the church with the Christmas tree.

Prayer

Heavenly Father, thank you for the birth, life, death and resurrection to eternal life of your Son, the Lord Jesus Christ. Help me to worship you as I prepare for all that I must do as a leader in your Church over Christmas. Amen.

Y

Young people

Since its inception, the Youth Service has a history of working with poor and disadvantaged young people. In the war years Macalister Brew (1943) described these young people as 'B' and 'C' graders with a sprinkling of late developers who had not yet caught up with others in mainstream education. In the 1960s, the *Albemarle Report* said that the first duty of the Youth Service was to the section of society that got least out of their schooling. The report highlighted the needs of the one million 15–18-year-olds who lost all touch with education as soon as they left school.

And so it has been since then, with the Youth Service largely focusing its resources on young people whose social and educational needs are not met elsewhere. Youth movements do not develop in those societies where the family can adequately prepare the youngster for life as an adult in the community. In such societies, there is no need for a separate Youth Service.

When the Church imports these assumptions into her work with young people she creates a deficit narrative for her youth work. The Church thinks of what she can do for young people, but not of what they can do for her. Young people are seen as being in a passive role needing to be told the gospel or to be helped to deal with difficult social circumstances. Voluntary sector agencies commend themselves to funders as being able to work with the hard-to-reach young people and the success of the youth work project is measured in inverse proportion to the social disadvantage of the young people before the work began.

Stories become self-fulfilling prophecies of themselves. According to the stories that are told of them, young people are a problem or an ally. In Czechoslovakia they became allies in the ending of communism. In his famous essay, *The Power of the Powerless*, written in Czechoslovakia at the height of communism, Vaclav Havel argued that young people should be called 'students' rather than 'dissidents'. Calling young people 'dissidents' made communism the norm and young people the outsiders; calling young people 'students' made them the arbiters of their own destiny. It is a distinction that was to have a significant effect on young people's self-perception. From then on they were able to help drive the process that led to the collapse of communism in 1989.

The message of the enigmatic, misunderstood Christ is that our teachers are those whom we least expect. The gift young people bring is the chance for us to form relationships with our previous selves and to learn from them. I find a searing honesty in Tanya who has argued with her father. He has got angry with her and she has walked out of the house. As she and I talk she exclaims in a mixture of frustration and despair, 'I am 15 and all I have got is this wall.' There is a dignified and lonely courage shown by Aamir who, at 21, is told that he is adopted and that the people that he thought were his parents are not.

When treated with respect young people become the allies the Church needs to find her place within a fast-moving and complex society. I have had a lifetime of building-based and detached youth work, church youth work and individual conversations and I have always found myself learning as much from young people as I am able to teach them. Young people are not a 'missing generation', but are just in a different place from where we expect them to be. They are not hostile to the Church, but are willing to engage with authenticity on any level.

Young people and death

Even without any previous church affiliation, young people still want the Church to exercise its traditional role of providing a ritual for death. Samuel, a young person in secondary school, is slashed, stabbed and killed outside the school. The young people look to me to help to provide them with a liturgy for death and to assist them in processing their feelings about what has happened. The church building provides a sanctuary for them to gather, light a candle, pray or simply be together.

Silence and story are two things that I can offer. The young people grab at words to create a shared identity through what has happened. I plan an open microphone session for young people who knew Samuel to gather together, tell stories and talk about what they are feeling. Stories enable people to own their confusion, but silences will allow them to move beyond their immediate grief. Job's friends provided most comfort to him when they did not say anything, but instead just listened (Job 2.13).

Words punctuate the silence. The significance of the liturgy in the funeral service is not just in the words, but in the silence it employs. It allows people to find their own level of meaning. I stand apart from their initial stages of their mourning. It is only if the young people are able to recognize that I am not a part of their immediate landscape of grief that they will be able to draw strength from what I have to offer. Therein lies the skill of the priest; it is the ability to know what can be done as well as what cannot be done.

Young people and church

Making links across generations is at the heart of a parish church's identity. Young people are helped to appreciate the social rules and values of the adults, with whom they interact in the community. Older people have the opportunity to hear the hopes and aspirations of young people whom, without the church, they would never otherwise have met. A church with healthy relationships with young people is a church comfortable with herself.

Jesus is an advocate for cross-generational learning:

> Then people brought little children for him to place his hands on them and pray for them. But the disciples rebuked them. Jesus said, 'Let the little children come to me, and do not hinder them, for the kingdom of heaven belongs to such as these' (Matt. 19.13–14).

There are two parts to the Kingdom of God being made up of children (Matt. 19.14). One is that the trust that children put in adults is a prototype of the trust that we are to put in God. The second is that the simplicity of a child's thinking models how we are to behave with one another. In the words of T. S. Eliot, the Christian faith is a condition of complete simplicity, costing not less than everything. All we need to say is simply 'Yes' or 'No' (Matt. 5.37).

A parish church is a multi-generational learning community. There are three stages of cognitive development – credence, criticism and conviction – that shape the learning of each generation. Credence is when the child accepts what his parents tell him. Criticism is when the young person is working through the issues for himself. Conviction is when the adult has reached the conclusions that he wants to adopt for himself. The Church is at her best when these different stages of learning are absorbed in a single conversation. Richard (aged 16) tells me that if he does not hit back when people bully him at school, the bullying will never stop. At this stage of the conversation he wants me as a companion alongside him, not an adult simply telling him that hitting others is wrong.

The strength of a multi-generational church in her work with young people is also her weakness. It needs people to work harder at relating to one another than they might do in a more homogenous group. Adults have to give space to those of a different generation, but there is no reason given in Scripture why they should not do so. According to the logic of the labourers in the vineyard (Matt. 20.1–16), there is no credit due to a longstanding church member simply by virtue of them being so. A conversation between an 18-year-old student and an 80-year-old widower – where each is not sure what to say to the other – exemplifies the fragile nature of Christian truth where each is reaching out to understand the other.

The traction of an age-specific or single demographic group is that young people can be drawn towards a faith in Christ without having to change their learning style or cultural group. I run an afternoon service for young people who play football on a Sunday morning and hence are unable to come to church. They arrive bursting with energy and swapping stories about their game that morning – one young person comments 'It's wicked! You can play football and have your own service.' Another says, 'I can really learn here. It's not like at church where people are going on and on and on.' There are key features that need to be absorbed into a church structure that enables young people to have their say:

1 Relationship-based rather than activity-driven

A desire to be true to oneself is integral to any young person's emerging sense of self. It is personal authenticity rather than religious authority that is the key guiding principle for young people. They respond to a church leader as an individual rather than to the role he occupies. Relationships are central to a young person's identity and authenticity in their decision-making. Collins-Mayo, Mayo and Nash (2010) write that young people shape their decision-making through a secular trinity of relationships with their family, friends and reflexive self.

Knowing what practical difference a belief might make is critical in how young people relate to the faith. For young people, authenticity means action and decision. They have a natural concern for issues of justice. This gives to the Church an opportunity to build on her natural strengths in how she relates to young people – a love of others and a concern for justice. God is hardwired as a God of justice.

Jesus' ministry was relationship dependent, and if his was, how much more so does that of a church need to be. Jesus' miracles always happened in the context of a relationship between him and the other person. Jesus' miracles were done in response to faith rather than in order to create faith. When he taught in his hometown synagogue they did not believe what he was saying about himself because they saw him only as the carpenter's son. They had no faith in him and he could not do any miracles there, except lay his hands on a few sick people and heal them (Mark 6.5–6).

2 Question-driven teaching

Jesus taught in an interactive manner, suited to a young person learning to find her place in the world. He taught by asking questions: 'Who do you say I am?' (Mark 8.29). He reached conclusions through dialogue (Matt. 12.11): 'If any of you has a sheep and it falls into a pit on the Sabbath, will you not take hold of it and lift it out?' He told stories: 'A farmer went out to sow his seed' (Luke 8.5).

Stories help young people to interpret and make sense of what happens to them and work out their responses. Stories of the faith allow young people to explore Christian belief at their own pace. In the wider society young people's attitude to the Church is increasingly one of benevolent indifference. We don't have to win over a hostile public, but to explain ourselves to an indifferent public. It is easier these days to get people to listen, but harder to get them to understand the Christian faith. As more and more evidence emerges that people know less and less about the Christian faith the task of the local church community becomes a consciousness-raising exercise before it becomes a truth-telling exercise.

The most thorough-going learning experience is to convey an idea to others; thus it is that in modelling Christianity to young people we learn it for ourselves. We who have grown used to the faith have become accustomed to using words such as 'ought', 'should' and 'must'. A young person finding her way in the world teaches us to relearn the grace at the heart of our faith. We avoid being drawn too quickly into a language of duty and obligation. Young people can be our teachers and will give as much to us as we will ever give to them. I don't ask young people what they want to be in their lives. I ask them what they want to change. The Church overlooks her precious jewels when she thinks of what she can do for young people, but not of what they can do for her.

Reflection

I am taking a funeral of a young mother who has committed suicide. Her 12-year-old son Daniel is sitting in the front row of a packed church and looking at me intently. For my address I speak to him directly. I tell him the story of Daniel and the lion's den. I say to him that he is in his own lion's den, but in the years to come he must remember that I, the priest at this his mother's funeral, had told him that when his morning comes he will walk out of his den with the lions looking on. I tell him that the despair he feels at his mother's death will be replaced by a determination to live his own life. In the church there is one young person listening and a congregation of 100 people looking on. Everyone is taking their cue from him. The stillness of how he listens to me affects everyone and as I speak you can hear a pin drop. He has become the teacher in helping others to absorb the reality of his mother's death.

Prayer

Dear God, help me to pay as much attention to those younger than me, as they always have to do to those older than they are.

Z

Zeitgeist

The Church has been an agent of her own marginalization in wanting to frame the discussion about Christianity in a manner consistent with a free market rationale of individualism and choice. In a desire for people to be able to respond to the gospel in terms of their own understanding, the Church has been happy to talk about the faith as values rather than truth, and as choices rather than story.

Consumerism is the social and economic ideology that encourages decisions on the basis of individual choice and preference, and is all-pervasive in how we understand the world. Professor Michael Sandel in the Reith Lectures in 2009 talks about how we have changed from a 'market economy' to a 'market society'. He cites the example of how financial payments have turned civic responsibility into a purchasable commodity. For instance, fines for parents who were late in picking up their children from school resulted in parents arriving later still. The financial payment had left the parents feeling that they were entitled to an after-school childcare provision.

The cross of Christ fits no worldview but its own. It is a stumbling block to Jews and foolishness to Gentiles (1 Cor. 12.3). When the Church bases its mission to society on the basis of shared values and common interests it is attempting truth without crucifixion. Jesus tells his disciples to love one another (John 13.35). However, this is Jesus telling them about the need for actions to substantiate words. Jesus was not suggesting to his disciples that all they needed to do was to draw on Christian values to open up a debate.

Christian values may improve people's social circumstances, but they will not transform their hearts. Improvement is a personal betterment. Transformation is a death with Christ in order also to live with him (Rom. 6.8). Truth is to be found only by relating oneself to Christ; and that he is the centre around which the unity of mankind here in history is to be built.

It is not possible to ride the horse of rationality and jump horses at the last moment and attempt to convince people that God's truth was revelation all along. The glorious clumsiness of a parish church cannot be explained away as cost-effective or representing value for money. My 150-year-old parish church building shows that some things only make sense when seen in the light of eternity.

We are a society in need of a story

A decline in the number of people going to church reflects a wider shift in patterns of social behaviour. Peter Berger (Berger, 1967) talks of plausibility structures, the network of people, traditionally family friends and neighbours who believe the same thing as us. The less people live within networks of belonging, the more important individual choice becomes because there are fewer points of reference. Putnam (2000) writes that we have become increasingly disconnected from family, friends and neighbours. He calls ours a 'post-associational society'. People's lack of connection with the Church is a part of a wider pattern of social disengagement. With fewer social determinants, people's prime point of reference becomes themselves and so what they want becomes all-important. Authenticity becomes an important guiding principle for Generation Y young people (Collins-Mayo, Mayo and Nash, 2010, p. 23).

In the absence of what Lyotard (1979) calls a 'grand narrative', people draw on a variety of different narratives to satisfy their need to feel a part of a wider whole. On a global scale, the Olympics and the World Cup every four years offer a sense of identification. On a national scale, Thanksgiving in America, Burns Night in Scotland, or Remembrance Day in England offer a sense of national identity. On an individual level, Lacan (2004) suggests that desire is an individual narrative and is fundamentally a desire for recognition. The significance of desire is the desire for significance.

As in all best conversations, *The Parish Handbook* ends where it began. The Introduction established the parish church as being relevant to society because of the counter-cultural nature of its activity. Here we return to the same idea. The Church gathers people together because it points to a world beyond which is the eschatological in-breaking of God's Kingdom. Luke has Jesus invoking the tradition of the messianic banquet as he begins his last meal with his disciples: 'For I tell you, I will not eat it again until it finds fulfilment in the kingdom of God' (Luke 22.16).

When God comes to us he does so in story. We are shaped as the people of God by stories and metaphors. Mayo, Savage and Collins (2004) write that over 75 per cent of the Bible consists of stories. Adding poetry and proverbs leaves probably less than 10 per cent abstract 'intellectual' content. It is precisely the stories from the Bible that help us to interpret and make sense of what happens to us and work out our responses.

In essence, stories are developed to reassure people and to make them feel a part of a wider whole. People want to place their own experiences in context. As humans we construct our own sense of self through the interpretations we place on the events and the meaning we give to realities around us. McFadyen (1990) describes social life as enacted narrative: 'I can only be said to know who and what I am because there are others who can be said to know who and what I am.' Individuality is formed through the way people make sense of the world: what the stories are that they tell about the experiences that have happened to them.

The parish churches are well placed to provide the story for which society seeks. The incarnation is a completing drama. It is a story of love, betrayal and heroism. The revolutionary Christian story is acted out week by week in local parish churches. Worshippers commit themselves to making new relationships and remaking existing ones in the name of Christ.

The light and fuel of a parish church's mission lies in the energy and creativity of its storytelling. The art of storytelling draws people into a wider whole and makes a community out of an otherwise unrelated group of people. The task of mission and evangelism is to connect the narrative of Jesus Christ with the many different narratives in which people live their lives and through which they find purpose. Stories appeal to people's imagination. When we tell a story we invite those listening to read themselves into the narrative and to take part in its outworking. We inhabit stories – Who am I? What do I consider to be important? What am I going to do about it?

It is through this sharing, relating and co-opting of stories of faith that the Christian story forms the church community which, in turn, shapes the character of the Christian believer, who is no longer conforming to the pattern of this world, but being transformed by the renewing of the mind (Rom. 12.2). Sally McFague writes:

> [For] the Christian, the story of Jesus is the story *par excellence*. For his story not only is the human struggle of moving toward belief, but in some way, that story is the unification of the mundane and the transcendent . . . [It shows us] God's way of always being with human beings as they are, as concrete, temporal beings who have a beginning and an end – who are, in other words, themselves stories (McFague, 1975, pp. 125 and 139).

Evangelism comes when we choose to share our stories with others so that they too can decide whether or not they want to keep it as their own.

Different people have different stories of their faith. One person's story may be changed in an instant through a personal conversion. For another person, conversion to Christ may take place over a number of years.

My favourite time to run is at 6 a.m. on an early winter's morning. There is never one single moment when the light changes, but at the end of the run I am able to appreciate that it has become wholly day. In a similar manner, belief in Christ will for some be a gradual process, and for others a single moment in time.

The Church provides a critical seed bed for the imagination out of which new ideas can emerge. If things were so different in the past when God became man, then they can be different in the future as the Holy Spirit takes root in people's lives and we await Christ's return.

Reflection

We stand at the edge of the most stunning landscape on which we have ever feasted our eyes. What is more, we are about to step in. We have never witnessed this before. It is the future. We can only see ahead, not behind; whatever came before is the past, from which we are set free, because we are invited to work through any consequences with our Lord Jesus Christ.

We are real-life, real-time players in today's most important story; it is Acts of the Apostles Volume II. From this day on we can kindle stories with others in the Jesus-centred family, as we become the anti-individualist revolutionaries of today, providing nutritious fodder for the inspiration of the saints of tomorrow.

How exciting to be selected to feature in the scenes of the new zeitgeist: the generation who travelled together in Christly discipleship. No one is left behind; all eyes are on the prize ahead: eternal corporate worship of the victorious Lamb.

Prayer

Thank you, heavenly Father, that you grant me freedom to be the story of Jesus in my era. Fill me with your Holy Spirit that I may walk confidently in the honourable position of service to those whom I am called. Help me to counter the culture, which sears at the true human heart, which is found only in our relationship with you.

Reflections and glimpses ahead . . .

THE RT REVD DAVID GILLETT

Excited by parish ministry? For me that's been one of the renewing features of reading through this book written by one of my former curates. It has been a joyful outworking of a narrative theological approach: the Bible is first and foremost a story – specifically God's story and his dealings with humanity as we see it lived out in the local parish church. The Bible's authority lies not so much in it being a set of propositions as in the story of God – God who is the loving Creator of all. And as God's story it has the power to change and direct all that we are and do. Time and again we return to the narrative itself and discover how it informs our life as a parish church today and how specifically we inhabit that story.

Narrative theology is content to leave the story as story. We are happy not to jump too quickly to a definitive conclusion, which applies to all people at all times. God deals in various ways with different people in the Bible's story. So univocal theological positions are not to be sought here too quickly – we need a more nuanced approach. God's stories fit us in appropriate and sometimes contrasting ways. And narrative theology is content to leave contrasting stories on the table for the dialogue to continue.

In his introduction to the Old Testament, Walter Brueggemann warns us not to assume that there is only one answer to a question when we are studying a particular passage or subject in the Scriptures. There has been a tendency for the Church in many periods to want to deduce universal rules that apply to all people's behaviour for all time. This has led too often to the desire to unchurch others. Brueggemann laments 'the pervasive Western, Christian propensity to flatten, to refuse ambiguity, to lose density,

and to give universalizing closure . . . Classical Western theological discourse, wants to overcome all ambiguity and give closure in
the interest of certitude' (Brueggemann, 1997, pp. 81 and 82). At
times the Church has been too ready to use our theology and our
system of ethics to exercise power over others. As both a principal
of a theological college and a bishop, I have been only too aware
of this temptation!

As we look at Scripture in this way we adopt an open approach
to others who seem to inhabit God's story in a slightly different
way from how we fit in. So we become a more generous people;
we welcome the advice not to develop 'an unhealthy interest in
controversies and quarrels about words that result in envy, strife,
malicious talk, evil suspicions and constant friction' (1 Tim.
6.4–5). We are slow to criticize and censor. This creates a parish
church that is ready to offer the hospitable open-handed grace of
God to a needy world.

A parish church: stable and changing

From the Patristic period through to the Reformation, the motto
of the Church was *semper eadem*, always the same, unchanging.
A common post-Reformation tag has been *semper reformanda*,
always being reformed. A strapline that reflects the approach of
The Parish Handbook could be *Ecclesia semper eadem et semper
reformanda* – a Church that owns joyfully the rhythms of 2,000
years of Christendom while looking expectantly for ways forward
amid the challenges of our society.

The Anglican parish church, celebrated in this handbook, has
at its heart the rhythm of daily prayer and regular eucharistic
celebration which links it vertically with the Church in history
and horizontally with today's Church around the world. We
enjoy the rhythm of the Church's year and we relax into the ongoing retelling of God's story. We rejoice in the patterns left in the
biblical story of regular celebrations. From the faithful in the Old
Testament, we value the pattern of pilgrimage to the temple for
the main festivals. As Christians, we continue those patterns with
our own festivals that have evolved over two millennia. Year by
year we enter in slightly different ways into that story. We inhabit

the story of Jesus as he withdraws to the mountain regularly to pray, and we seek to model similar patterns in our own lives. On the other hand, we are thankful that we can sit with the disciples in the Garden of Gethsemane because we too fall asleep and fail to watch with Christ as he intercedes for us. We are glad that the parish church is always the same – more or less.

But then there are those times when we face something entirely new, a challenge that maybe knocks us sideways. The crisis looms and we learn how to face radical change.

Think of a cluster of five rural parishes suddenly faced with the prospect of losing their parish priest. They are to be joined with the neighbouring parish that is already in a team with two other villages. Perhaps the model of the Hebrew believers travelling from their own villages up to the temple in Jerusalem three times a year offers a new story-pattern for them. In terms of our own English history, we are returning to an earlier chapter of our story when small congregations lived at a distance from their minster church where the priest(s) would be based. Then we would likely have been visited occasionally by a wandering friar – none of those for our emerging story today.

But now with universal education, and the gifts of modern technology, we are able to make different provision for parishes that live dispersed around their central minster church. Lay ministers will normally provide the teaching in the local parish with the team rector celebrating the Eucharist every so often in their church. She will quite probably provide the framework of Christian nurture, but much of it will be delivered by members of the congregations. Hopefully parish churches are learning fast the value of lay ministry as the primary resource within the parish. This resources not only its social involvement, but also the retelling of the story and providing Christian nurture. It is also the time to recognize the vital contribution of priests who have retired from stipendiary ministry often with 15–20 years of healthy active life ahead of them. They are not simply people to 'fill in' when nothing or no one else is there. Their experience is often vital to the flourishing of the local parish church. And in many places there are far more 'retireds' than 'non-retireds'.

But for some – priests or laity – such irruptions to routine can come as an overwhelming challenge. It becomes a time when their very faith is knocked back to its roots. Their world is falling apart, the stresses of the new are too great, and prayer seems no longer the stable resource it has always been. The old familiar story in which we have lived for so long with others has failed us.

It is time to find a radically fresh story. Maybe the flight of Elijah into the wilderness is a story to inhabit (1 Kings 19). Like him, to acknowledge the depth of panic and despair which has suddenly overtaken and destroyed all the familiar landmarks that the inherited rhythms have provided. The regular cycle of the Church's year and the patterns of prayer and retreat are not enough. This is a once in a lifetime crisis where something radical is needed. Elijah's 40-day trek into the wilderness, like the '40-pattern' in the story of Moses before and Jesus later on, is what is needed. Maybe the radical break of staying for a month or two in solitude in a lonely cottage somewhere will be the appropriate step to take. Or, as I discovered, five weeks walking the Camino de Santiago de Compostela, in Spain, was part of the process of dealing with loss – two years after my wife had died.

On the Camino I became friends with a lawyer from Latin America whose wife had told him to leave his practice and go on the Camino for two months to recover from the dreadful effects of stress at work. Both of us found God in that – as did Elijah on the mountain. For me, as for the prophet, God was found in 'the sound of sheer silence'. For Elijah, it came as he sat through the demonstration of God's awesome power, only to hear God in the sheer silence of his presence. For me it was in the inner silence created by the rhythmic monotonous tread of my boots on the track as I recited the Jesus prayer for several hours most days in time with my walking: *Lord . . . Jesus . . . Christ . . . have . . . mercy . . . on . . . me . . . a . . . sinner.*

But silence is not only vital when things crash. This handbook has shown along the way why silence, waiting, aloneness and stillness are vital as part of the rhythm and change of each parish church. I recall important words of Michael Ramsey, the hundredth Archbishop of Canterbury – probably even more crucial now than when he wrote them half a century ago:

Intercede does not mean to speak or to plead or to make requests or petitions: it means to meet someone, to be *with* someone in relation to or on behalf of others. Jesus is with the Father for us. And our prayer means essentially our being with God, putting ourselves in his presence, being hungry and thirsty for him, wanting him, letting heart and mind and will move towards him; with the needs of our world on our heart. It is a rhythmic movement of our personality into the eternity and peace of God and no less into the turmoil of the world for whose sake as for ours we are seeking God. If that is the heart of prayer, then the contemplative part of it will be large. And a Church which starves itself and its members in the contemplative life deserves whatever spiritual leanness it may experience.

Bigger stories still to come . . .

The parish church, which this book has presented, is exciting because it can grow and flourish in so many contrasting ways. Three strands within the Bible story evoke some of the excitement of what it means to be the ongoing story of God today – Prophecy, Wisdom and Apocalyptic.

The *Wisdom* tradition occupied centre stage within the Bible's story for about a thousand years, mostly recalled in the books of Proverbs, Ecclesiastes, Job, Wisdom, some of the Psalms, and in the teaching of Jesus, especially the parables. Scholars have often seen this Wisdom tradition as central to an Anglican approach to life. It encourages reflection, is non-judgmental and non-credal. It puts a high priority on *Shalom*, peace and order. It finds expression in the parish church's commitment to liturgy and all things done 'decently and in order'. Events and traditions, which are seemingly quite ordinary, suddenly and unexpectedly open up to what is quite extraordinary.

It is the honest folk wisdom that so typifies many parish churches – the local farmer who has been church warden for years and has a deep instinct for how God relates to both land and people. He gives witness to a Creation faith and our duty to care for the environment. Or the schoolteacher, whom God uses over many decades to nurture a living faith in generations of children and young people. She has brought an understanding of God and given stable foundations of faith that have endured through countless crises in individual lives.

It is also this Wisdom tradition that helps the parish church relate well to other faith communities. It speaks of the universal truths that most of the great world religions share – especially within the Abrahamic faiths. We share with Jews and Muslims a belief in the one Creator God, the value of every human life, and a concern to model the values of God's rule in our daily lives. Working from this Wisdom-based faith we can appreciate, and indeed learn, from one another; we can strive together for the common good; and we can unite in working for peace between our communities both here and around the world.

This handbook has rejoiced in the Wisdom tradition at many points: it is a valuable charism within the Anglican parish church. It offers the invitation to inhabit God's 'peace, which passes all understanding', a good that many are anxiously seeking in the stresses of their lives. It is a feature of the parish's mission that is arguably more valuable now than in previous generations. But, if allowed to dominate, this Wisdom tradition has its dangers. The scribes who wrote and preserved it in ancient Israel supported the status quo. They were serving the good order of the king. And as such it is a tradition that can be used to dominate others, stifle initiative, or outlaw anyone who seeks to 'rock the boat'. This very gift can become a tool for the manipulator, the control freak, or the power-hungry. However, it is a great benefit when the parish has one or two who dare challenge when the leader – ordained or lay – begins to love the Wisdom tradition too much and exemplifies some of these dangerous character traits.

The *Prophetic* aspect of the Bible story counterbalances the prophetic. It proclaims 'Thus says the Lord!' It calls people to radical action. It bewails the absence of social justice. It demands that the community of faith remedy the situation; that the widow, the orphan, the refugee and the outsider are cared for and treated with equal worth and dignity. The prophetic impulse of the parish church is to work for liberation and justice. It will be open to adventure and exploration.

How daring is the parish church to enter into the story of the prophets and listen as Amos rocks the boat? 'I hate, I despise your religious festivals; your assemblies are a stench to me' (Amos 5.21). Beautiful liturgy and music honour God and support mission, until they become ends in themselves, or trophies of pride that proclaim the specialness of that particular parish. Never easy to hear such messages! And it is too easy to look to others when the prophet says, 'Hear this . . .' you 'who oppress the poor and crush the needy' (Amos 4.1). The parish church can be the eyes and ears of the community. Others may turn a blind eye and deaf ear. The prophetic within the Church will be searching out such needs.

The prophetic also resources our interfaith engagement. It challenges the blind and fearful fundamentalisms that can evolve within any religious tradition. It questions any faith community where human rights are denied and trampled on, sometimes in the guise of religious or spiritual principles. It searches people's inner motivations to expose prejudices such as anti-Semitism. It highlights one faith community's intolerance of another in the past so that honest open relationships can be built today.

As with the other two strands within the biblical story, *Apocalyptic* adds to the breadth of a church's vision. We discover this strand mostly in the books of Daniel and Revelation, in some apocryphal works, as well as in some chapters of the Gospels. It speaks mainly to the situation where the faithful people of God are facing dark times and insuperable odds. At such times the reasoned approach of the Wisdom tradition or the bold proclamation of the Prophetic fail to meet the imminent threat.

There are church communities in other parts of the world that are beyond the stories created through wisdom and prophecy. Only the intervention of God provides the answer and they live in expectation of divine deliverance. Seeing this, some in our part of the world adopt a similar apocalyptic analysis of the secularizing society in which we live. It is not uncommon for the Church to feel under threat and persecution when laws are passed that seem to erode the protection that Christianity has enjoyed in the past. But this requires the response of wisdom and prophecy, not the cry of terminally threatened believers.

However, there are ways in which we in Britain need to inhabit the apocalyptic story, for apocalypse transports us to where we often fear to tread. It evokes the poetic and visionary within the Church. It points our minds first to the future, which God has planned for the whole world. We see today in the light of tomorrow. The Eucharist is seen as a joyful foretaste of the great banquet of heaven, and not only a feeding on what Christ has done in the past. Our worship becomes an opening up to the heavens and an unashamed desire to share the wondrous reality of God with our neighbours. We rejoice to know that all wrongs will be put right and God will be all in all. We are gripped by the vision of God. The story of the parish church could hardly get more expansive than that!

Bibliography

Adirondack, S., 1998, *Just about Managing? Effective Management for Voluntary Organisations*, London: London Voluntary Service Council.

Archbishops' Council, 2014, *From Anecdote to Evidence: Findings from the Church Growth Research Programme (2011–2012)*, London: Church House Publishing.

Beck-Gernsheim, E., 2002, *Reinventing the Family*, Cambridge: Polity Press.

Berger, P., 1967, *The Sacred Canopy: Elements of a Sociological Theory of Religion*, New York: Doubleday.

Borgman, D., 2013, *Foundations for Youth Ministry: Theological Engagement with Teen Life and Culture*, Grand Rapids, MI: Baker Publishing.

Bosch, D., 2003, *Transforming Mission: Paradigm Shifts in Theology of Mission*, New York: Orbis Books.

Bosch, D., 2006, *Witness to the World: The Christian Mission in Theological Perspective*, Eugene, OR: Wipf and Stock Publishers.

Bretherton, L., 2010, *Christianity and Contemporary Politics: The Conditions and Possibilities of Faithful Witness*, Oxford: Blackwell.

Brierley, P., 2014, *UK Church Statistics, Number 2, 2010 to 2020*, Tonbridge: ADBC Publishers.

Brueggemann, W., 1989, *Finally Comes the Poet – Daring Speech for Proclamation*, Minneapolis, MN: Augsburg Fortress Press.

Brueggemann, W., 1997, *Introduction to the Old Testament: The Canon and Christian Imagination*, Louisville, KY: Westminster John Knox.

Brueggemann, W., 2007, *Mandate to Difference: An Invitation to the Contemporary Church*, Louisville, KY: John Knox Press.

Brueggemann, W., 2014, *Sabbath as Resistance: Saying No to the Culture of Now*, Louisville, KY: John Knox Press.

Brunner, E., 1934, *The Mediator*, Cambridge: Lutterworth Press.

Chartres, R., the Right Reverend, 2015, *Boydell Lecture*, delivered at Inner Temple Hall.

Chesterton, G. K., 2011, *Orthodoxy*, Hollywood, FL: Simon & Brown. First published 1908.

Cocksworth, C., 2008, *Holding Together: Gospel, Church and Spirit*, Norwich: Canterbury Press.

Collins-Mayo, S., Mayo, R. and Nash, S., 2010, *The Faith of Generation Y*, London: Church House Publishing.

Crossley, M., 2000, *Introducing Narrative Psychology: Self, Trauma and the Construction of Meaning*, Buckingham: Open University Press.

Davie, G., 2007, 'Vicarious Religion: A Methodological Challenge', in N. Ammerman (ed.), *Everyday Religion: Observing Modern Religious Lives*, New York: Oxford University Press, pp. 21–35.

Davie, G., 2008, 'Debate', in S. Wells and S. Coakley (eds), *Praying for England: Priestly Presence in Contemporary Culture*, London: Continuum.

Dewey, J., 1933, *How We Think*, Buffalo, NY: Prometheus Books. First published 1910.

Donovan, V., 1982, *Christianity Rediscovered: An Epistle from the Masai*, London: SCM Press.

Dostoevsky, F., 1991 edn, *Crime and Punishment*, London: Penguin.

Dulles, Avery Robert Cardinal, 2005, *A History of Apologetics*, San Francisco, CA: Ignatius Press.

Earey, M., Lloyd, T. and Tarrant (eds), 2009, *Worship that Cares: An Introduction to Pastoral Liturgy*, Norwich: Canterbury Press.

Eliot, T. S., 2001, *The Four Quartets*, London: Faber and Faber.

Etchelles, R., 1972, *Unafraid to Be*, Nottingham: Inter-Varsity Press.

Fernandez, E., 2006, 'The Church as a Household of Life Abundant', in Darby Kathleen Ray (ed.), *Theology that Matters: Ecology, Economy and God*, Minneapolis, MN: Augsburg Fortress Press.

Foucault, M., 2006, *History of Madness*, New York: Routledge.

Freire, P., 1970, *Pedagogy of the Oppressed*, New York: Continuum.

Frost, M. and Hirsch, A., 2003, *The Shaping of Things to Come: Innovation and Mission for the 21st Century Church*, Peabody, MA: Hendrickson Publishers.

Fukuyama, F., 1992, *The End of History and the Last Man*, London: Penguin.

Fung, R., 2002, *The Isaiah Vision*, Geneva: World Council of Churches.

Genz, S., 2001, *The Social God and the Relational Self: A Trinitarian Theology of the Imago Dei*, Louisville, KY: Westminster John Knox Press.

Handy, C., 1988, *Understanding Voluntary Organisations*, Harmondsworth: Penguin.

Harvey, D., 1992, *The Condition of Post-modernity*, Oxford: Blackwell.

Hauerwas, S., 1981, *A Community of Character*, Notre Dame, IN: University of Notre Dame Press.

Hauerwas, S. and Gregory Jones, L. (eds), 1990, *Why Narrative? Readings in Narrative Theology*, Grand Rapids, MI: Eerdmans.

Heelas, P. and Woodhead, L., 2004, *The Spiritual Revolution: Why Religion is Giving Way to Spirituality*, Haboken, NJ: Wiley-Blackwell.

Hervieu-Léger, D., 2000, *Religion as a Chain of Memory*, New Brunswick, NJ: Rutgers University Press.

Herzog, W., 1994, *Parables as Subversive Speech: Jesus as Pedagogue of the Oppressed*, Louisville, KY: Westminster John Knox Press.

Higginson, R., 1996, *Transforming Leadership*, London: SPCK.

Hunt, S., 2003, *Anyone for Alpha?*, London: Darton, Longman and Todd.

Inge, J., 2003, *A Christian Theology of Place: Explorations in Practical, Pastoral and Empirical Theology*, Surrey: Ashgate.

Jackson, R., 2002, *Hope for the Church*, London: Church House Publishing.

Jamieson, A., 2002, *A Churchless Faith: Faith Journeys beyond the Churches*, London: SPCK.

Lacan, J., 2004, *The Four Fundamental Concepts of Psycho-Analysis*, London: Karnac Books.

Lewin, A., 2009, *Prayer Is Like Watching for the Kingfisher.* Norwich: Canterbury Press. Used by permission.

Lewis, R. and Lewis C., 1983, *Inductive Preaching: Helping People Listen*, Wheaton, IL: Crossway Books.

Lloyd, T., Earey, M. and Tarrant, I., 2007, *Connecting with Baptism: A Practical Guide to Christian Initiation Today*, London: Church House Publishing.

Lyotard, J., 1979, *The Post Modern Condition*, Manchester: Manchester University Press.

Macalister Brew, J., 1943, *Informal Education*, London: Faber and Faber.

Macintyre, A., 1990, *After Virtue*, London: Duckworth.

Mackintosh, H., 1927, *The Christian Experience of Forgiveness*, New York: Harper and Brothers.

Malbon, B., 1999, *Clubbing: Dancing, Ecstasy and Vitality*, London: Routledge.

Martin, D., 2002, *Christian Language and its Mutations: Essays in Sociological Understanding*, Theology and Religion in Interdisciplinary Perspective Series, London: Routledge.

Mayo, E., 2010, *A Dog Helps Dog World*, Manchester: Co-operatives UK.

Mayo, B., Savage, S. and Collins, S., 2004, *Ambiguous Evangelism*, London: SPCK.

McFadyen, A., 1990, *The Call to Personhood*, Cambridge: Cambridge University Press.

McFague, S., 1975, *Speaking in Parables: A Study in Metaphor and Theology*, London: SCM Press.

Moltmann, J., 2008, 'God in the World – the World in God: Perichoresis in Trinity and Eschatology', in R. Bauckham and C. Mosser (eds), *The Gospel of John and Christian Theology*, Grand Rapids, MI: Eerdmans.

Murray, S., 2004, *Church After Christendom*, Carlisle: Paternoster.

Newbigin, L., 1976, *A Local Church Truly United*, Geneva: WCC.

Newbigin, L., 1982, 'Cross-currents in Ecumenical and Evangelical Understandings of Mission', *International Bulletin of Missionary Research*, vol. 6, pp. 146–51.

Newbigin, L., 1986, *Foolishness to the Greeks: The Gospel and Western Culture*, London: SPCK.

Newbigin, L., 1989, *The Gospel in a Pluralist Society*, London: SPCK.

Newell, R., 2010, *The Feeling Intellect*, Eugene, OR: Wipf and Stock Publishers.

Nouwen, H., 1975, *Reaching Out: Three Movements of a Spiritual Life*, New York: Image Books.

Nouwen, H., 1997, *The Inner Voice of Love*, London: Darton, Longman and Todd.

Oakley, M., 2016, *The Splash of Words*, Norwich: Canterbury Press.

Okechukwu Ogbonnaya, A., 1998, *On Communitarian Divinity: An African Interpretation of the Trinity*, St Paul, MN: Paragon House.

Pattison, S., 2000, *Shame: Theory, Therapy, Theology*, Cambridge: Cambridge University Press.

Percey, E., 2014, *What Clergy Do: Especially When it Looks like Nothing*, London: SPCK.

Percy, M., 2004, 'Losing our Space, Finding our Place', in S. Coleman and P. Collins (eds), *Religion, Identity and Change: Perspectives on Global Transformation*, Aldershot: Ashgate.

Pope Francis, 2013, *Evangelii Gaudium: The Joy of the Gospel*, Vatican City: Vatican Publishing House.

Pritchard, J., 2007, *The Life and Work of a Priest*, London: SPCK.

Putnam, R., 2000, *Bowling Alone*, New York: Touchstone.

Regan, J., 2002, *Toward an Adult Church: A Vision of Faith Formation*, Chicago, IL: Loyola Press.

Richard, L., 2000, *Living the Hospitality of God*, Mahwah, NJ: Paulist Press.

Rylands, M., 2006, 'Mission-Shaped Cathedrals', in P. Bayes and T. Sledge (eds), *Mission-Shaped Parish: Traditional Church in a Changing World*, London: Church House Publishing.

Saint-Exupéry, Antoine de, 1975, *The Little Prince*, Wordsworth Children's Classics.

Savage, S., 2006, *The Future of the Parish System: Shaping the Church of England for the 21st Century*, London: Church House Publishing.

Schnabel, E., 2005, *Early Christian Mission*, Leicester: Inter-Varsity Press.

Sheldrake, P., 2001, *Spaces for the Sacred*, London: SCM Press.

Simkins, T., 1977, *Non Formal Education and Development*, Manchester: Manchester Monographs.

Stott, J., 2006, *The Cross of Christ*, Westmont, IL: Intervarsity Press.

Tavinor, M., 2007, in P. North and J. North (eds), *Sacred Space: House of God, Gate of Heaven*, London: Continuum.

Taylor, C., 1992, *The Ethics of Authenticity*, Cambridge, MA: Harvard University Press.

Thatcher, A., 2007, *Theology and Families*, Oxford: Blackwell.

Tillich, P., 2010, *The Eternal Now*, London: SCM Press.

Tomlin, G., 2009, *The Provocative Church*, London: SPCK.

Vanier, J., 1989, *Community and Growth*, Mahwah, NJ: Paulist Press.

Vanstone, W., 1977, *Love's Endeavour, Love's Expense: The Response of Being to the Love of God*, London: Darton, Longman and Todd.

Voas, D. and Crockett, A., 2005, 'Religion in Britain: Neither Believing nor Belonging', *Sociology*, 39(1), pp. 11–28.

Volf, M., 1996, *Exclusion and Embrace: A Theological Exploration of Identity, Otherness and Reconciliation*, Nashville, TN: Abingdon Press.

Von Rad, G., 1973, *Genesis: A Commentary*, Louisville, KY: Westminster John Knox Press.

Wallis, J., 2013, *On God's Side: What Religion Forgets and Politics Hasn't Learned About Serving the Common Good*, Oxford: Lion Books.

Warren, Y., 2002, *The Cracked Pot: The State of Today's Anglican Parish Clergy*, London: Church House Publishing.

Watts, F., 2001, 'Shame, Sin and Guilt', in A. McFadyen and M. Sarot (eds), *Forgiveness and Truth*, Edinburgh: T & T Clark.

Weil, S., 2001, *The Need for Roots: Prelude to a Declaration of Duties Towards Mankind*, London: Routledge.

Wells, S., 2006, *God's Companions*, Oxford: Blackwell.

Williams, R., 1995, *A Ray of Darkness*, Lanham, MD: Cowley Publications.

Williams, R., 2000, *Christ on Trial: How the Gospel Unsettles Our Judgment*, Grand Rapid, MI: Eerdmans.

Williams, R., 2014, *Being Christian*, London: SPCK.

Wright, N. T., 2003, *Resurrection and the Son of God*, Minneapolis, MN: Augsburg Fortress Press.